DOLLS' HOUSE
MAKEOVERS

DOLLS' HOUSE MAKEOVERS

Jean Nisbett

PRINCIPAL PHOTOGRAPHY BY ALEC NISBETT

GUILD OF MASTER CRAFTSMAN PUBLICATIONS LTD

First published 2001 by
Guild of Master Craftsman Publications Ltd
Castle Place, 166 High Street,
Lewes, East Sussex BN7 1XU

Text © Jean Nisbett 2001
© in the Work GMC Publications 2001
Line drawings by John Yates
Cover photographs: © Mulvany & Rogers (Palace of Sans
Souci, top left; Hampton Court Palace, bottom right) and
Alec Nisbett
Other photographs © Alec Nisbett, and see
Acknowledgements, page 148

ISBN 1 86108 206 1

Edited by David Arscott
Book and cover designed by Ian Hunt Design

Set in Giovanni Book and Frutiger

Colour origination by Viscan Graphics (Singapore)
Printed and bound in by Kyodo Printing (Singapore)
under the supervision of MRM Graphics, Winslow,
Buckinghamshire, UK

CONTENTS

for
Ian, Mark and Bertie

INTRODUCTION

Whether you wish to create a modern home, a grand period room or a background to show off a specialized collection of miniatures, this book, with its pictured examples in many different styles, is a practical guide to achieving the perfect setting.

Designing a room and choosing colours to make a suitable background for the contents are skills that can be learned. Some of my own early houses were redecorated several times before I was satisfied, and in my later, more ambitious houses the rooms have been rearranged from time to time as my ideas have developed and I have recognized the opportunity to try something new.

Fortunately a miniatures makeover is not nearly as disruptive or expensive to achieve as in a full-size home. Reinvent your dolls' house: take a fresh look at period decorations and alter any room which, on reflection, you feel is too bland. Research your new interest thoroughly before you begin and you will enjoy creating something totally unlike anything you have attempted before.

In a modern room you can use vivid colours and expensive-looking materials which might not suit your family home but which you would expect to find in luxury hotels and apartments or in exotic locations around the world. In the smaller scale you are free to decorate in any style you choose, without having to consider such practical constraints as whether the materials will wear well.

The cost of our hobby also needs to be considered, and in this book the emphasis is for the most part on economy. There are suggestions for the use of cheap (sometimes even free) materials to provide wall and floor coverings, and on ways in which to achieve unusual decorations using crayon or pen. Hints are given on where to find paints which work well on

ABOVE *Real fruit is arranged as a centrepiece to give an indication of the room size in this ornately gilded replica of the marble hall from the Palace of Sans Souci in Germany. It would be difficult to match these superlative painting skills, but such settings can provide a rich source of ideas for schemes that may be more modest both in cost and skill required.*

RIGHT *This beautiful Islamic room is both exotic and inspirational. The window frames are panelled in limewood, stained and handpainted like the originals from which they were copied. The floor is a combination of individual tiles and painted panels, assembled to make the design. The sofa is cast in resin from a hand-carved master.*

small surfaces and which are widely available in sample sizes.

Practical work is covered in detail. Throughout the book you will find examples of unusual furniture to make, and the finished pieces are pictured in appropriate room settings to show the effect they can have. In Chapter 7 there are contrasting 'before' and 'after' examples, showing cheap furniture which can be reassembled and transformed by repainting, and this section further demonstrates how to achieve a professional finish on furniture made up from kits.

As a contrast there are also pictures of unique craftsman-made furniture and a selection of both grand and simple rooms which have been decorated by leading makers working in the miniature scale. The decorative ideas and techniques they employed may provide inspiration for your own thoughts on the perfect room, at whatever level of skill you may be able to achieve.

If you want to experiment with an original idea which is very different from the regular dolls' house room, it will work best if you devise a simple setting. Chapter 4 is devoted to settings arranged in room boxes – an inexpensive alternative to a complete dolls' house. They save space, and for anyone with limited time they represent a satisfying manner of completing a smaller and more specialized interior.

A room box also offers opportunities to try out ideas which may have been unsuitable for your first dolls' house, perhaps to decorate in period style after completing a modern interior or vice versa. In a one-room setting you will be able to experiment with any style without the need to relate to the more orthodox rooms of a whole house.

The final chapter summarizes techniques which the newcomer to the hobby will find useful, and it will act as a reminder to the more experienced. It details appropriate paint colours for period rooms, lists the basic tools you need and, for reference, includes diagrams showing basic techniques.

DECORATION AND DISPLAY

RIGHT *A room decorated in a formal style can be intimidating, but the elegant pink salon from the Palace of Sans Souci has a welcoming and homely atmosphere. China and a silver kettle-on-stand on the small table suggest that tea is about to be served.*

There are two main kinds of dolls' house hobbyist: those for whom decorating and making miniatures is an end in itself, and those who prefer to concentrate on collecting. Inevitably, these interests overlap. Most hobbyists, however addicted to making, like to include some professionally-made miniatures in their rooms, while it would be an unusual collector who did not wish to display attractive miniatures in a suitable setting.

In a period room the architectural details should be correct and the colour schemes appropriate or the effect will be spoiled. In a modern room innovative schemes can include up-to-date designs and simulate new materials.

As you buy or make additional miniatures, you may find that some reorganization is necessary. If the decorations already seem perfect it would be a pity to replace them: a simple rearrangement of contents may suffice. Our tastes change, often influenced by current styles of interior decoration, and (as with a real home) renewing the wallpaper or paint colours will sometimes be quite enough to give the room a refreshingly new look.

You may, however, choose to transform the room completely, and there are many ways in which you can achieve this. I here give some examples of changes which will create a different appearance and atmosphere in otherwise similar rooms.

How to arrange your miniatures will depend on whether you want a homely interior or one that will show off a collection as a formal display. An art gallery or antique shop are examples of more formal settings which can work well.

Consider the effect you wish to achieve, but also imagine how this will complement the miniatures you intend to include. Take time to plan the room, and also think about the period.

Collect materials whenever you see them: build up a stock of useful papers, fabrics and other materials for future use. Don't limit yourself to specially scaled-down versions of the real thing, although these may be best for a period room. After a while the magpie habit will become second nature to you.

It is worth saving braids and ribbons, lace edgings and gift ties, buttons and jewellery bits and pieces, wallpaper and fabric samples. Giftwrap and pictures from greetings cards are especially useful for modern rooms. The more oddments you have to choose from, the more likely – and the more easily — you are to arrive at an unusual and interesting scheme .

ABOVE *In this comfortable, early nineteenth-century room all the furnishings have been carefully selected for the use and pleasure of the supposed occupants. The wallpaper has been cut and pieced from leftovers of a full-size pattern.*

ABOVE *A spacious hall in an early Victorian house, presented as part of a lived-in home, with evidence of family activities and hobbies.*

ABOVE *A later version of the Victorian entrance hall now appears as a formal reception area. The major decorative change is to the flooring. Wallpaper and festoon blind remain the same.*

ABOVE *This small shop room measures only 9in (230mm) deep, 10¼in (260mm) wide and 8in (200mm) high. The display space is devoted to dolls' houses which are in 1/144th scale, the right size to suit a 1/12 room.*

ABOVE *The same display space is again used to the full in this second version, where it has been transformed into a modern, up-market kitchen shop. There are 120 miniatures in this room without it looking overcrowded.*

ABOVE *This first version of my interior design shop could almost be used as a sitting room. In time, however, the collection of miniatures increased until it warranted a complete rearrangement.*

ABOVE *In this later shop layout the decorations are unchanged, but the arrangement gives a completely different impression. Which of the two do you prefer?*

CHOOSE A COLOUR SCHEME

Start with a basic premise and a selection of colours to choose from. Try out colours using paint sample pots, which are inexpensive and available in most modern paint ranges. For the period room, look at a shade card of authentic historic colours.

If you want to create your own colours do some trial mixes with acrylic paint or artist's gouache and water-based emulsion paint. You will need only a few drops in a neutral base to achieve vivid effects.

As you will know from decorating your own home, a shade can look different in daylight from how it appears in artificial light. Colours also change according to what is placed next to them, and this will be particularly noticeable in the small space of a dolls' house room.

Paint a sample on card and fix papers or fabrics with Blu-tack or double-sided Scotch tape to judge the effect before making a decision. The results may surprise you, and it is worth taking a look at several combinations before you finalize the scheme.

It is also worth building up a collection of cuttings from magazines as reference if you plan a modern room or one from a country other than your own.

ABOVE *The painted decoration simulating marbled panels and floor in this stunning room was based on schemes shown in paintings from the early Renaissance. The floor is painted on a resin base, which gives an exceptionally smooth surface. The door is heavily gilded.*

Do not follow ideas slavishly: rather, use them as a starting point. In Chapter 5, to provide additional inspiration, I show miniature rooms which feature decorations from different parts of the world to prove that unusual colour combinations can look good.

LEFT *A room setting based on the Parrot Room in Sturehov, near Stockholm, elegantly furnished with Gustavian-style furniture. The colour scheme and painted panels look their best in clear Swedish light, which is often reflected by snow through the large windows.*

FIREPLACES

Most rooms benefit from having a focal point and, even where there is central heating or in a warm climate where the nights may nonetheless be cold, this may well be a fireplace. Choose it carefully, as it will set the tone of the room.

Some very fine miniature fireplace surrounds are made in cast resin to reproduce the elaborate detail, and they may be a good choice for a period room. Plainer ones ready for you to paint yourself are surprisingly inexpensive, while fully-finished versions complete with marble or painted surrounds and fitted with grates are available to suit most periods.

You may prefer to make your own period fireplace in wood, which can be painted to simulate marble. Instructions for making a basic fireplace surround are given on page 11.

Modern fireplaces are easy to make, as there is usually no need to mitre and fit any additional mouldings. 1950s and 1960s fireplaces dispense with a mantelshelf as a rule, and have a tiled finish which can be simulated in card. Some more recent designs also use tiles, and mantelshelves are coming back into favour.

ABOVE *The fireplace in an early Tudor home was used both to provide heat and for cooking. A spit to roast meat and a variety of blackened metal pots and griddle plates add realism.*

ABOVE *A heavily carved 'stone' fireplace from the sixteenth century features heraldic shields to emphasize the importance of the house owner.*

ABOVE *A chimneypiece based on a design by William Kent suits a formal eighteenth-century room with black-and-white tiled floor. This cast design has a green marbled inset and a black metal period fender. Instead of a fire, a painted chimneyboard (a picture cut from a magazine) has been fitted.*

ABOVE A pretty chimneypiece with carved decoration which would suit a late Georgian, Regency or early Victorian room. Brass fender and firearms and an Adam-style grate complete the effect. This fire surround is made in cast resin.

LEFT In a continental room a tall, woodburning stove, rather than an open fire, may be used to provide heat. This handpainted Swedish stove is a replica of an eighteenth-century stove from the famous Marieberg factory in Stockholm.

ABOVE This fireplace was made to suit a late twentieth-century Chinese room (shown on page 70), and uses card and paper over a plain base made from oddments of wood. Shiny, white-patterned card provides a modern tiled effect. Instructions are given on page 65 to make a slightly different version.

MAKE A BASIC FIREPLACE

A plain fireplace can be made from three pieces of wood moulding mitred at the corners, as shown on page 86.

Mouldings designed specially for fireplaces are available, but many architrave mouldings are suitable, too.

A basic fireplace made from plain stripwood can be built up with additional plain or fancy mouldings to make a more elaborate design, and a mantelshelf can be added. (See pages 46 and 56-57.)

To complete the fireplace, mount on card backing with an aperture cut out for the grate. Glue on ceramic tiles or marbled card to make a surround. Back the aperture with matt black card and glue the entire fireplace to the wall.

HINT

A simple way to make two fireplaces is to remove the glass and backing from a small picture frame and cut the frame in two. It may be of wood, leather or resin, any of which can be painted satisfactorily.

ABOVE *Planning a fireplace design before assembly. Some mouldings have been painted to show the different styles used, and the pieces are temporarily Blu-tacked to card.*

BELOW *The finished effect.*

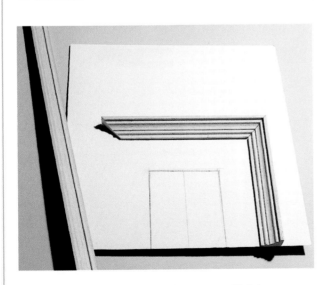

ABOVE *A simple fireplace which was assembled from cornice moulding left over from another project. The height of the finished fireplace should relate to the height of the room: experiment with a cardboard cutout before you decide what will look best.*

WINDOW DRESSING

Think about the period you wish to replicate. Tudor houses did not at first have glazing in the windows (rudimentary wooden shutters could be closed in order to keep out the wind and rain), whereas late Tudor windows had leaded glazing, supplemented by heavy curtains or tapestries.

Eighteenth-century curtain arrangements helped to define the style of the room and could be either plain white muslin or extravagant drapes. The Victorians added blinds, which were lowered to keep out strong sunlight or to provide privacy. For the dolls' house, such minute quantities of fabric and trimmings are needed that you can afford to use real silk, which will hang well at small windows. Synthetic fabrics have a tendency to stick out, and will not drape well in short lengths.

ABOVE *An unglazed window on a timber-framed house looks on to a storeroom. Cool air would have helped to keep the food fresh.*

ABOVE *In this long room the two many-paned windows have floor-length curtains made from acid yellow Indian silk trimmed with thin gold braid. The draping is based on a Regency example.*

ABOVE *Shorter windows in an early nineteenth-century room are fitted with lace fixed blinds and ruched pink silk festoon blinds. This arrangement neatly solves the problem of deciding on curtain length.*

USE DISPLAY SPACE TO THE FULL

Make sure that all your miniatures can be clearly seen. Any flat surface will serve to display accessories, ornaments and domestic equipment. Mantelshelves and tables are obvious places, but cupboards can be left open to show their contents. Alternatively, you may want to keep tiny items in a drawer – both to stop them rolling away and to create an additional surprise when the drawer is opened.

Dresser shelves can hold a matching dinner or tea service, or a mixture of pottery. The earliest dressers combined a low side table with shelves fitted to the wall above, but before very long this arrangement was amalgamated into a single piece of furniture.

A dresser will fit into most period or modern rooms, as it has never gone out of fashion: today's upmarket country kitchen often boasts a pine dresser filled to overflowing with modern or antique spongeware.

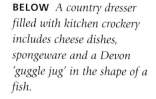

BELOW A country dresser filled with kitchen crockery includes cheese dishes, spongeware and a Devon 'guggle jug' in the shape of a fish.

BELOW A collection of pewter miniatures shows to advantage against darker oak. You can cram on as many pieces as possible without spoiling the effect.

LEFT *A willow pattern dinner service and a set of mugs in a different design but also in blue-and-white, arranged on a traditional Cotswold-style oak dresser.*

BELOW *The elegant Regency chiffonier has a similar function to the dresser. The tea service is pewter, handpainted in vivid yellow, while the pleated green silk on the cupboard fronts conceals some of the contents.*

BELOW *The dresser shown on page 14 is now filled with a collection of Staffordshire figures and cookware. Even the top is put to use, showing off lidded jars and vases.*

MAKING FOOD

The food shown here was made by professional miniaturists, but you can make plain food yourself, using one of the modelling compounds which is hardened in the oven. Start with apples, oranges and potatoes to practise the technique before you try something a little more ambitious, such as a cake, chicken or pineapple.

To achieve the most realistic effect, use neutral-coloured modelling compound (instructions for use are provided with the pack) and after baking, paint with model enamels. Mix colours to achieve the exact shades you want.

BELOW *Victorians paid great attention to the presentation of food. The table was covered with either white damask or a lacy cloth, while an elaborate floral arrangement or small nosegays in front of each place setting added to the effect. The centrepiece on this supper table combines flowers with a moulded jelly 'shape'.*

ABOVE *Dessert could be laid on separate small tables, always (in Victorian times) with a floral centrepiece.*

COLOUR MIXES

● Apples can be made to look edible by painting in green, yellow or orange shades to give a russet effect. Add a dot with a black fineline pen at the centre top.

● Oranges are easy too. Use a wooden cocktail stick to rough up the surface of the paint a little before it dries, to create the peel effect.

● Potatoes for the kitchen or storeroom look realistic if, once the paint is dry, they are dabbed with glue and rolled in instant coffee powder to simulate earth.

ABOVE *Simple food: whole cheeses mature on a plain wooden table.*

ABOVE *A Tudor banquet may include oysters, a gilded pie, wooden bowls of potage, roast peacock and a boar's head centrepiece. The oranges have been added for effect, not authenticity.*

RIGHT *Bread, fish and vegetables were staples of the medieval diet, with meat as a rare treat. The fish and bread on this plain table are made of wood and handpainted.*

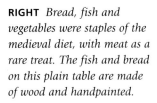

ABOVE *A Regency supper of fruit, syllabubs, nuts and wine could have been served as a light repast during an evening's entertainment. A glass epergne, fruit stand and decanter add sparkle to the table while the wine is kept cool in a brass-banded mahogany wine cooler.*

ABOVE *Picnic food! A Japanese lunch box or sushi laid on a board are unusual, and would work well in a modern interior.*

ABOVE *A well-scrubbed pine table shows food being prepared in a Victorian kitchen. A wooden spice tower and a brass sugar sifter are ready for use.*

FOOD STORAGE: OPEN PLAN

Before the advent of the refrigerator, even modest homes had a walk-in larder. This was used to store crockery, pans and preserves, and sometimes wine and cider, as well as perishables which needed to be kept cool.

A separate larder in a small room next to the kitchen will allow you to show off a quantity of food and crockery, not only on shelves but perhaps also by using the floor. Should your dolls' house have no convenient room adjacent to the kitchen, consider partitioning off a section to use as a larder. A door-frame and a non-opening door can be fitted on to the partition wall to suggest access.

BELOW *This larder has a floor of 'Welsh slate' cut from a magazine picture. For more realism, use miniature roofing slates, cut square, or ceramic flagstones.*

BELOW *A corner for flower-arranging is a useful feature in a country larder: an old cupboard is often used so that vases can be stored below the work surface. This inexpensive cupboard has been stripped and repainted to simulate a distressed finish. (Full instructions are given on page 141.)*

HOW TO MAKE A LARDER

Plan your larder carefully, working out the position and depth of the shelves to suit the miniatures you want to put on them. Provide a wide shelf at the back and at one or both sides for dairy produce, meat and fish, then narrower shelves above for pots, pans and preserves.

There is no need for fancy joinery in a utility room, so keep it simple. The side shelves can be butted up against the ones at the back, and the wood left unpainted to give a clean and well-scrubbed look. The bottom, wider shelf can be about 3in (75mm) from the floor to allow space below for bottles, flagons and wine-making equipment, vegetables and bulk stores in baskets, sacks or tubs. Oddments of wood strip can be used for the shelves, and shaped or angled pieces will provide shelf-supports.

1 Decide on the width of the lower shelf and cut from stripwood. At the back of a typical larder in 1/12 this might be 1¾in (45mm) deep, and the shelf at the side might be narrower. Adjust the measurements in order to suit your own particular requirements.

2 Cut supports for the back shelf from ½in (12mm) square dowelling and glue in position. Glue the shelf onto the supports and to the wall.

3 Cut a support for the side shelf and glue to the wall and floor at the front of the larder. An extra ½in (12mm) thick support can be added to the wall under the centre of the shelf. Glue the shelf on top of the support and to the wall.

4 The upper, narrower shelves can be glued to right-angled triangular or plain woodstrip supports and then glued to the wall.

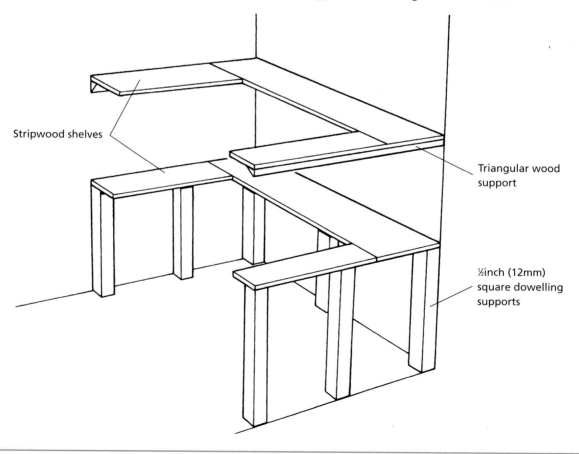

Stripwood shelves

Triangular wood support

½inch (12mm) square dowelling supports

FURTHER IDEAS FOR OPEN STORAGE

● Provide a linen cupboard in a bedroom, bathroom or on a landing. For a country effect, arrange piles of neatly folded linen on the shelves. Cut cotton fabric to the exact width of the shelf to be filled and long enough to fold over several times. Crease and press lightly before tying with very thin ribbon.

● Make use of luggage. Maximize the potential of a trunk or suitcase by showing what is inside: it would be a waste of space to keep the lid fully closed. The contents can be arranged neatly or left to spill out. You might like to put some folded clothing nearby to suggest packing in progress.

BELOW *Make the most of fresh-looking linen. A bed need not be made up with all the sheets and blankets covered but can be used to show them off.*

ABOVE *A red leather trunk with removable shelf and the traditional fitted lining of thick flowered paper. The contents include a piece of tiny handworked flower embroidery which was originally part of a fine Swiss handkerchief.*

ABOVE *A nicely made wardrobe can be used to store linen, and a drawer provides additional space to be filled. Leave the door open to show off your textile collection.*

ABOVE *The Japanese have learned how to use limited storage space to the full. Stepped shelves are used for this scaled-down version of a Girls' Festival Display with a traditional arrangement of dolls and miniatures in a strict hierarchy. The Emperor and Empress are at the top, with court ladies and ministers below and, at the bottom, tiny representations of furniture and food.*

RIGHT *An example of early furniture designed for storage, this Tudor highbacked settle has a hinged seat. It has been left open to reveal folded coarse linen in shades of ochre, which could be produced by using natural plant dyes. Before the invention of the hanging wardrobe, clothing was also folded and stored in this way, and herbs were strewn in the folds.*

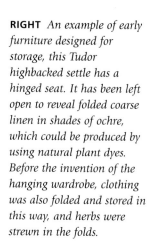

First impressions

The first glimpse into a dolls' house before it is opened up is through the windows or a doorway. Even a small window will reveal some of the delights inside. Try to arrange the contents so that there is something interesting to see when you look in.

An open doorway or a passage can be equally enticing. A through-passage separating the hall from kitchen and buttery was a common feature of early Tudor houses. Placing a garden feature at the far end will enhance the period atmosphere.

An entrance hall or porch needs as much attention as the main rooms. It sets the scene for the style of the house, whether simple or grand.

The hall should reinforce the impression you wish to create, just as it would in real life for a visitor entering the house.

RIGHT *A pair of 'stone' lions to guard the entrance establishes that this is a wealthy household, so we know that the rooms inside will be well-furnished.*

RIGHT *A window opening from the balcony of a Venetian palazzo is heavily latticed but allows a glimpse of the room inside: the feeling of anticipation is immediate.*

RIGHT *A stone mullioned window offers a view through into a Tudor kitchen with wooden tubs and baskets of vegetables. Strong iron bars keep out intruders.*

ABOVE *This striking hall was copied from Powerscourt, an Irish country house. The unusual design of the plasterwork ceiling features shells, which were cast in resin from a hand-carved original. The deer heads feature branching antlers which were all carved individually so that no two are alike.*

ABOVE *The theme of this house is sunlight, with the representation of the sun over the porch, carved in wood by the maker but painted as stone. The stained glass window with its echoing rays provides both light and reflected colour.*

ABOVE *The sunlight theme is continued in the entrance hall, panelled in mahogany and spruce, where the sun's rays appear over a doorway. The gilded metal balusters on the staircase typify the Art Nouveau influence.*

Carry through whichever theme you choose. A Georgian hallway, for example, would have a side table. In a Victorian house, you might install an umbrella stand beyond the door for authenticity, while an Edwardian home should perhaps be given a hallstand for coats, hats and umbrellas, and a small modern home might include a bicycle or a pushchair in the hall.

A typical cottage interior is small, and a traditional cottage will have a thatched roof and tiny windows, making it difficult to see inside. One option (see below) is to have a lift-up roof which will give a good view into the upper rooms. This works well and is just as exciting as opening the front.

RIGHT *Windows let in light and help to illuminate the richly painted and gilded stucco decorations of this miniature of the Ante-Collegio from the Doge's Palace in Venice. The space between the windows is taken up by a monumental fireplace.*

ABOVE *The entire thatched roof of this flint and brick Oxfordshire cottage is hinged at the back so that it can be lifted up to give good access to the upper rooms. The main lower front opens in the centre.*

PERIOD ROOMS

RIGHT *The elaborately decorated Sala Regia in the Vatican provides a superb setting for a banquet. This reproduction includes the work of several leading miniaturists. The table is laid with gold plate, and more of the service is displayed on a heavily carved dresser, all illuminated by chandeliers and branched candelabra.*

2

RIGHT *The magnificent throne room from Hampton Court Palace contains the work of a number of miniaturists. An extravagant chandelier and torchère illuminate seventeenth-century Delftware tulip vases, tapestries and the richly upholstered throne itself.*

We all have our favourite historical period and can imagine the type of room we would like to re-create in miniature, whether it is oak-panelled from the age of Henry VIII, a Regency room which might have been lived in by Jane Austen or a Victorian room filled with ornaments.

Many hobbyists concentrate on grand rooms, partly because a peasant room with an earth floor seems to offer little scope for decoration and cannot be filled with a collection of fine miniatures. Well-filled rooms are a legitimate objective, but even an empty room can give a great deal of pleasure.

ABOVE *This austere interior needs no furniture to add to its beauty. It is based on a Saxon church in Berkshire, England. Light streams in through the doorway, and additional illumination is provided by cartwheel candle lights which are electrified.*

If you love ancient buildings, you might find it equally enjoyable to create the impression of age and history by trying out distressed paint finishes and including the bare minimum of furniture.

RESEARCH YOUR CHOSEN PERIOD

If you plan a period setting, it is best to be authentic. Unless you are already an expert on your chosen period, it is essential to do some research to avoid anachronisms. You may also like to suggest the way in which a room has been used over the generations, by decorating in a style to suit the architecture but including furniture and accessories of a more recent time, just as we do in real life.

Begin, if you can, by visiting a preserved historic house to look at the details at first hand. In Britain it is possible to tour houses from most periods, and European countries are generally rich in buildings which reflect regional vernacular styles. In America, New England has some lovely eighteenth-century houses which are open to the public, and there are early houses in many other states, too.

The next best thing is to consult one or more of the many books which are devoted to period styles in decoration and furnishing. My own initial sources of inspiration lie in British interiors.

TUDOR

Basic decoration of Tudor rooms is simple: plastered walls can be colour-washed in off-white or ochre. Other possibilities include exposed timbers or oak panelling. The floors should be either 'stone' slabs or wide oak planks.

For the walls, simulate plaster with water-based emulsion paint, thickened a little with some interior filler if you want a rough finish. As a slightly patchy effect is authentic, one coat will probably be enough. In a room where all the walls are left uncovered you might also choose a deep pinky-red or yellow ochre, traditional colours which give a rich effect.

Internal timbering often works best if used on one or two walls with the others as plaster. In a real Tudor house the timbers, such as the ceiling beams, formed part of the frame construction and were both heavy and strong. Adding them on afterwards is not good building practice but looks fine in miniature, and it means that thinner woodstrip can be used.

To add timbers, use woodstrip approximately ⅛in (3mm) thick and ½in (12mm) wide and distress

ABOVE *Timbers on a plastered wall combine with an oak screen to give this room an ancient appearance. Ceiling beams run from front to back so that they can be seen clearly.*

ABOVE *Tudor brickwork was masterly. This replica of part of the old kitchen in Gainsborough Old Hall, Lincolnshire, is a faithful copy of the original. For the hobbyist, using brick cladding in sheet form is the easiest option, but for those with patience miniature bricks can be laid in courses and grouted in. In smaller domestic rooms brickwork was usually plastered over.*

ABOVE *This magnificent roof was made by a craftsman skilled in the restoration of full-size roofs, and was constructed using pegged joints in the traditional way. The windbraces form an elaborate pattern of curving oak which delights the eye.*

it by denting it at irregular intervals with a small hammer. Shave the edges of the wood here and there so that it is not perfectly straight. Colour with wood-stain to simulate oak before fitting.

Plan out the arrangement of the timbers using a picture of a real Tudor house as a rough guide to positioning. Cut the strips to size and glue in place.

Few of us can hope to emulate the elaborate roof structure shown above, but plain beams can be spaced across a ceiling, as was more general in smaller buildings. Use ⅝in (16mm) square dowelling (from a model shop), cut it to length, then distress and stain as before and glue in place.

ABOVE *Plain oak panelling with plastered walls above. In this case the upright and crosspieces are fitted over oak veneer, but a similar effect can be achieved by using inexpensive wood and distressing and staining before gluing in place.*

LEFT *In the seventeenth century, wall panelling became much more elaborate. Here is a splendid example of a Restoration room in the time of Charles II. Note also the elaborate design of the plasterwork ceiling. For the hobbyist, ceiling paper with a design simulating plasterwork can be glued on in a single piece (see page 105).*

PROJECT

How to fit wood panelling

1 First cut veneer or thin ply to fit the space that is to be panelled.

2 Cut a length of stripwood to fit along the base and a similar piece for the top of the panelling.

3 Mark out the placing for the uprights at approximately ¾in (20mm) intervals. They need not be spaced regularly, so this can be varied a little. Cut an upright to the required height, using a mitre block with a straight slot to ensure that the cut is straight at top and bottom to create a neat fit against the crosspieces.

4 Mark this first upright and keep it to use as a guide to cut all the others to the same length. Do not use the guide piece, as the others will be fractionally longer when cut.

5 Stain all the wood before gluing on, as woodstain will not cover any minute smudges of glue, which would show up as bare patches later.

HINT

Use light oak stain to give the impression that the house is newly built. Medium oak stain will make a pleasing contrast against plain walls and is my choice. Use dark oak stain if you want the house to look as though it is 400 years old and has darkened with age.

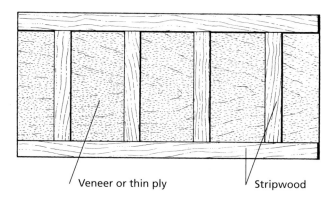

Veneer or thin ply   Stripwood

Furnishing

Tudor furniture was sparse. Wealthy home owners might have only one good bed, a chest for storage, one high chair and a number of joined stools and benches. Tables were often no more than boards which were set up on trestles at mealtimes. Servants slept on the floor and sat on benches.

Despite these limitations, the main rooms were designed to impress. The best furniture was richly carved and painted; tapestries and portraits of the owner of the house, his wife and important relatives were hung in gilded frames; and family crests, heraldic shields and weapons were displayed, often arranged to make an elaborate pattern on a wall.

Grand banquets were staged to impress influential visitors. Many courses of elaborately presented food were brought in by servants in procession, to the accompaniment of music performed on sackbuts, viols, shawms and other early instruments.

ABOVE *Even a king's room was not very comfortable, although he had the benefit of an impressive high-backed chair with a cushion.*

ABOVE *An upper servant might have to sleep in the storeroom and share the bed with one or two others. Sacking on the floor or, at best, a truckle bed would be usual, but in this room a low bed is provided as the height of luxury.*

ABOVE *Tudor rooms were full of colour. Use tapestries and other hangings, portraits, armour, pewter, candles and food to bring the room to life. In this scene, tapestries based on millefleurs French designs add warmth above the dais in the hall. The hangings, reproduced by a photographic process to look like scaled-down woven fabric, are surprisingly realistic when fitted in place.*

ABOVE *An oak cupboard is decorated with painted and gilded Tudor roses, which add colour to an otherwise utilitarian piece of furniture. A set of Scottish pewter drinking vessels and plates is arranged on top.*

ABOVE *The service end of a great hall, with separate entry and exit doors to the kitchen through the massive oak screen – to avoid confusion when courses were served and cleared. The musicians played in the gallery above the screen's passage.*

Economical Ideas for Tudor Rooms

● There is nothing more attractive than the sheen of real pewter, but if the dishes and plates are to be covered with food you can economize by painting card plates with Metalcote model enamel. This dries quickly and looks good buffed up with a soft cloth.

Mix two shades together to achieve the appearance of pewter: a combination of the shades representing aluminium and polished steel works well.

● Wooden buttons also make good platters. The holes can be hidden by food.

● Candleholders and tall candle stands obviously need candles. Making wax candles is time-consuming and difficult, but replicas can be made from wooden cocktail sticks. Cut to length and shave one end to a suitable shape to fit the holder. Paint with typewriter correction fluid or alternatively use a white marker pen: this is less messy than painting with a brush which then needs cleaning, and the fluid dries in minutes. In such a small size a wick is not essential, but if you do want to provide one, glue on a short strand of embroidery cotton.

● Downstairs floors can be of ceramic or resin flag-stones (glue on with a rubber-based glue such as Copydex). For economy, make your own flooring from thick card-board. Cut out some square and rec-tangular templates to use as patterns and cut plenty of each size. Make a card pattern to fit the floor, and glue on the 'flagstones', mixing the shapes randomly. Trim the edges neatly if they overhang the card base. Lastly, varnish with matt or semi-matt varnish and glue the floor in place in the room.

● Wooden floors should be planked. Real wood looks best in a Tudor room and, to be true to the period, it should be oak. Wood strip for use as dolls' house planking is available in several widths: choose the widest, which is about ¾in (20mm) wide. Cut a floor pattern in card as above, cut the planks to a variety of lengths and glue them on. Iron-on wood-strip is another option, provided it is of wood veneer and not synthetic material. Finish with a coat of matt varnish or, if the house is to be updated inside, use a satin finish.

● Shields decorated with heraldic devices will add colour. Transfers and metal blanks from a military model shop will give you a choice of coats of arms. Fix the shields high up on the walls for the best effect.

● Include some authentic early music instruments. A lute, a recorder or a shawm would be appropriate.

UPDATING THE TUDOR INTERIOR

Many Tudor houses of the grander sort are still lived in today. Try updating a Tudor room to present its panelled and beamed interior in a new way. In time the furnishings and decorations of each historical period come back into fashion: the 1920s was a time when Tudor once again became popular.

Imagine one wing of a Tudor house, formerly a parlour with solar above it, originally built around 1560 for the lord and his family. The fireplaces and oak panelling remain, but now planked floors are made more comfortable by adding Turkish carpets. Candles have given way to table lamps made from Chinese blue-and-white porcelain vases topped by silk shades with bobble fringes.

Upholstered chairs in Queen Anne style (winged chairs helped to keep out draughts before central heating was introduced) now supplement the oak benches and stools, but the 'country house style' arrangements would have delighted the Tudors, who loved their flowers.

ABOVE *In the 1920s and 1930s everyone wanted oak furniture (preferably darkened) and pewter tankards were displayed on heavily carved refectory tables and court cupboards. Additional comfort was provided by a reproduction Knole sofa.*

ABOVE *This miniaturized interior is typical of many which graced the pages of* Country Life Magazine *in England during the late 1920s and early 1930s. A fine eighteenth-century English japanned chest of drawers imitating Chinese style was a popular addition to such a room.*

ABOVE *The eighteenth-century-style dummy board soldier near to the Tudor fireplace is from two centuries later than its setting but not out of place in an updated room. Chinese porcelain was also admired and collected in the 1920s and introduced wherever possible. The Imperial yellow porcelain plate on the chimney breast is a rare treasure, and even rarer in a miniaturized version.*

IDEAS FOR THE UPDATED TUDOR ROOM

● Flower arrangements help to lighten an oak-panelled room. Use the tiny fabric flowers and leaves that are sold for trimming hats. These are longer-lasting than dried flowers and will not lose their colour. For the English country house look, make a trailing arrangement and set the container on top of a tall wooden plant stand.

● Work a small piece of embroidery on Aida fabric to display on an embroidery stand to represent work in progress.

● Dogs were always present in a country house, and one or two large ones will add realism.

RIGHT *An arrangement of yellow flowers and glossy green leaves shows up well on a plain oak chest.*

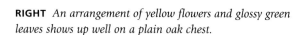

THE WILLIAM AND MARY INFLUENCE

Period styles in Britain are dated from the name of the reigning monarch, but new ideas took many years to reach country districts far from London, so there is always some overlap.

William and Mary reigned only from 1689 to 1702, but the style of decorations and furniture they introduced continued in favour through the Queen Anne and Georgian periods right up to the Regency, when the Prince Regent introduced new fashions.

Chinese wallpaper panels and lacquer furniture imported by the East India Company could add a

ABOVE *Walnut became the most used wood at the end of the seventeenth century: a William and Mary room may have a walnut floor as well as furniture. The Aubusson carpet in this room is of about the same date, while the torchère which illuminates the scene is an elaborately carved and gilded Italian Renaissance piece which even then would have been regarded as a treasured antique.*

ABOVE *The East Closet of Hampton Court Palace was designed in the late seventeenth century by Daniel Marot, a Dutchman. Although the room is panelled and floored in oak (reproduced in limewood in the miniature) it does not appear dark. Portraits, a marble fireplace and a carving (after Grinling Gibbons) are illuminated by a six-light chandelier.*

lighter touch to dark, panelled rooms. During the later Georgian period oriental lacquer was copied by English craftsmen using a technique which is known as japanning.

Another idea introduced by William and Mary was to include blue-and-white Delft pottery as a strong decorative element. Sets of five vases, known as Garniture de Cheminée, were commonly shown off on mantelshelves, with additional pots on brackets arranged on the wall (see page 101), while large tulip vases might stand in a window embrasure or corner, directly on the floor. Dutch tiles served as fireplace surrounds and to decorate dairies and stillrooms.

ABOVE *A japanned double chair with cabriole legs would be suitable in a late seventeenth-century room. The original of this chair is of a slightly later date.*

ABOVE *A William and Mary table made in walnut with floral marquetry decoration in many different woods. This lovely miniature is based on an exceptionally beautiful original table which was probably made in England.*

IDEAS FOR A ROOM SHOWING WILLIAM AND MARY INFLUENCE

● Colour the woodwork with walnut woodstain, and include the skirting boards. White paint became fashionable during the later Georgian period. Use Chinese wallpaper over a dado rail or, alternatively, inset into wooden surrounds as panels. The paper shown on page 37 was a sample for a full-size pattern, but miniaturized designs are available from dolls' house outlets.

● Blue-and-white miniature pottery and porcelain cover the range from top quality individual handcrafted work to inexpensive imported pieces.

● Choose portraits which show the correct costumes for the period and frame them with gilt picture-frame mouldings (see framing, page 86).

● Tapestries were still used to keep out draughts. In a bedroom a tall four-poster bed can have warm-looking woollen hangings.

● Firedogs (andirons) were used in fireplaces to support log fires: grates came into use during the Georgian period.

● Make a small scene to frame and hang, using miniature blue-and-white ceramic tiles which can be mounted on thin wood or card. Alternatively, cut out pictured tiles from a magazine or museum postcard, provided that they are to the right scale and are printed clearly.

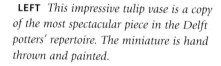

LEFT *This impressive tulip vase is a copy of the most spectacular piece in the Delft potters' repertoire. The miniature is hand thrown and painted.*

GEORGIAN STYLES

The English Georgian and Regency periods cover a wide variety of decorative styles and the reigns of four kings. In 1714 when the first George became king, domestic interior decoration was generally unostentatious. Rooms were painted in a limited range of colours: deep red, dull green, brown and even a shade known as 'drab' were used. Fireplaces were set into the painted panelled walls without even a mantelshelf.

'Georgian style' covers more than a century, and in the 1760s Robert Adam, the great architect who was also one of the first designer-decorators, instigated a huge change in decoration. Light blues and greens were picked out with white, and ceilings were often coloured pink. Gilded details were introduced, and beautiful carpets were laid over wooden floorboards which previously had been left uncovered.

Curtains of velvet and silk were draped in elaborate folds, and ruched blinds softened large windows. Fireplaces became much grander: the surrounds were made of marble if it could be afforded, or painted in simulation if it could not.

The type of decorations you choose may depend to some extent on the size of your budget. A room can be grand without being ostentatious: use paper to simulate richer types of material. Even curtains and a pelmet can be made of textured paper which can look and feel like fabric. The paper used inside a box of chocolates as packing can be suitable, as it is easy to form into pleats and drapes well. Once pressed firmly into place the folds will retain their shape, unlike many of the fabrics used for small-sized curtains.

Furniture in the Georgian room must be in keeping, or the whole effect will be ruined. The simple and unequalled elegance of an eighteenth-century room with just a few fine pieces of furniture is the very epitome of style.

LEFT *A Tower of the Winds was a Georgian folly favoured by owners of stately homes: there are still some in existence. This model is based on plans for one which was never built. The room features a handpainted marble floor with a complicated design to suit the octagonal shape of the room. The 1/144th scale model of the building is hinged to open, and is painted and decorated inside as an exact replica.*

LEFT *Georgian splendour: the magnificent saloon from Powerscourt, one of the great houses of Ireland, which was gutted by fire in the 1970s. This miniature re-creation contains eight Corinthian columns and twenty six Ionic pilasters, all cast in resin from hand-carved masters. The elaborate gilded ceiling and railings are faithful copies of the originals.*

LEFT *A Georgian hallway with a marble floor simulated in tiled flooring paper. The walls are painted in Adam blue. Two marble-topped side tables furnish the hall. The curtains are of textured paper.*

LEFT *An English eighteenth-century room furnished with a George I writing desk, a Hepplewhite shield-back chair and a Chippendale design with a heavily carved back splat and a seat of striped silk.*

LEFT *American furniture of the same period is equally elegant but gives a different effect. These Philadelphia chairs and table in black walnut date from around 1770. The table is designed to take up little space when closed, and is fitted with two gatelegs with which to extend the two deep flaps.*

LEFT *A delightfully curvaceous example of a double chair made in mahogany. The cabriole legs are similar to those on the japanned chair shown in the William and Mary section. (p. 38) The intricately shaped back splats need meticulous care in carving to ensure that both are identical.*

THE REGENCY

During the English Regency distinctive furniture and elaborate decorations were introduced by the Prince Regent, who became King George IV in 1820: after his accession the period is known as late Georgian.

The prince was fond of music, which was the most popular evening entertainment at the time. Your starting point for a music room could be a dolls' house wallpaper pack with a musical motif, which is widely available. The pack contains three plain sheets of wallpaper and one sheet printed with panels on a musical theme. There are more than enough panels to cut out and glue to the walls in the manner of an eighteenth-century print room. Smaller panels can be used to emphasize a doorway, mirror or window or on either side of a fireplace.

First paper the walls and leave to dry out. Mark the position of the fireplace, plan out an arrangement and fix the motifs temporarily with Blu-tack while you finalize the design.

ABOVE *The Regency connoisseur admired continental workmanship. The original of this Italian cylinder desk, with a Roman scene inlaid in marquetry on the front, might have been brought back and installed in a Regency study.*

ABOVE *Simple materials can be assembled to create an elegant effect.*

ABOVE *A Regency music room is a stylish setting for some fine furniture and musical instruments, which are here arranged for a soirée.*

ABOVE *Refreshments make an essential contribution to the success of a musical entertainment. A lyre-ended sofa continues the musical theme and a pedestal table is used to display dessert plates and a pyramid of fruit.*

Fix them in place using solid glue stick: you need apply only a little of this to each corner. Solid glue works well, as it is possible to shift the motifs around without marking the walls while you make sure that they are straight before pressing them firmly into place.

Furnish your room with Regency-style chairs for use both by performers and audience. The chairs can be ready-made or in kit form for you to assemble yourself. A chaise longue would have provided more comfortable seating for the most important lady in the assembled company.

Musical instruments for a Regency room can be a specialist maker's masterpiece or a readily available imported model, so for these you can spend as much or as little as you wish, to suit your budget.

At the top end of the range, an exact copy of a period instrument by a master craftsman will certainly be expensive, but it will repay the cost by giving you a lifetime's pleasure. Harpsichords and square pianos are both suitable for a Regency room, although the harpsichord had been superseded by the beginning of the nineteenth century.

LEFT *The centrepiece of this music room is the beautiful harp, made by an expert craftsman. The fine stringing and the use of pale, polished sycamore make it the focus of attention.*

ECONOMY HINT

An inexpensive harp can be transformed by painting and gilding. Instructions are given on page 141.

LEFT *The original of this square piano was made by the famous John Broadwood at the end of the Regency period. The miniature is made in Cuban mahogany with inlaid ebony stringing. The keywell is veneered in satinwood with rosewood crossbanding, and there are two brass grilles for sound.*

WALLS AND FLOORING

Painted walls are an option which will allow you to hang pictures rather than use a musical motif: yellow, Adam green or blue would be suitable. Buy a sample size pot of water-based emulsion paint in an authentic 'historic' colour for a really good effect. Make sure that your framed paintings continue the prevailing Regency theme.

The flooring used to suit the formal style of the room is a plasticized tile sheet which is easy to cut and lay in one piece. Trim to fit if necessary, and glue lightly round all the edges. Polished mahogany flooring would be another suitable choice.

Georgian-style skirting board and cornice were used throughout the Regency period, too, and make a neat finish to a room. Paint and fit skirting boards after the fireplace is glued in. Authentic scaled-down versions of Georgian skirting board give the best impression and should be mitred at the corner joins, as shown below.

An acceptable inexpensive alternative is to use plain stripwood approximately ⅝in (16mm) high and butt the corners together. Paint the skirting off-white before fitting.

Cornice should always be mitred at the corners. It is generally painted white but can be gilded for a decorative effect in a grand room

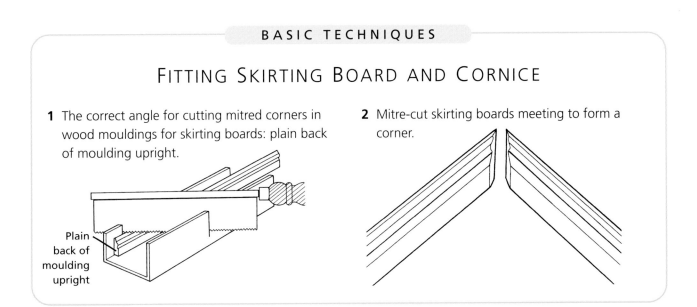

BASIC TECHNIQUES

FITTING SKIRTING BOARD AND CORNICE

1 The correct angle for cutting mitred corners in wood mouldings for skirting boards: plain back of moulding upright.

Plain back of moulding upright

2 Mitre-cut skirting boards meeting to form a corner.

ESSENTIAL FITTINGS

A fireplace is an important feature in the Regency room and can be made of painted wood. You will need some plain stripwood as a base and fancy mouldings for the top layer. On mine the mouldings were from a cut-down 1/12 door frame, reassembled in a different way. Reeded wood and square panels with a circular central motif were both featured on Regency fireplaces.

The size of the fireplace can be varied to suit the room. The one shown is 4in (100mm) high and 4½in (115mm) long, plus the mantelshelf. Before you fit the fireplace to the wall cut a piece of matt black card slightly larger than the aperture and glue to the back of the fireplace. Glue a strip of black card to the floor at the base of the aperture, and add a hearth of marbled card.

ABOVE *The completed fireplace is fitted with a purchased miniature Adam grate and a hearth of marbled card. The vase on the mantelshelf is a handpainted copy of a Regency design.*

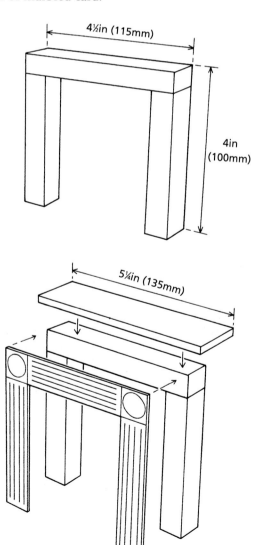

IDEAS FOR THE REGENCY ROOM

● Refreshments are important. Provide little pedestal tables to hold wine and glasses.

● A side table can be laid for a buffet supper.

● A pole screen placed near the fire is a useful and decorative addition.

● Include a music stand: sheet music for this can be handily reduced on a photocopier. For clarity, choose a sheet with few notes, perhaps a piece for a beginner. Or write your own, using a fineline black pen, and reduce it in size.

RIGHT *Pole screens could be moved easily to shield ladies' faces from the fire. Heavy make-up was worn, and it had a tendency to run if the heat was too intense.*

THE CONTINENTAL INFLUENCE

BELOW *A cabinet fillet with continental-style china and glass and a writing desk/bureau are both in the unmistakable Biedermeier style: these pieces were made from kits. The floor covering is a plasticized tile sheet which is ideal for this room style and would be suitable throughout the Victorian era which followed.*

Even before Victoria became queen of England in 1837, decorations were becoming more fussy. Floral-patterned carpets were introduced, curtains were made of rich brocade or velvet, and wallpapers were striped or patterned and topped with a border. Stencilling or handpainting was the latest way to add interest to floorboards.

The European equivalent of this style was known as Biedermeier, which roughly equates to bourgeois. Homes were much more comfortable for the average family, and you can be lavish with ornaments and accessories in the dolls' house room.

HINT

Silhouettes depicting family and friends were popular before cameras were in general use. Frame your own in jewellery backings.

ABOVE *This room looks more comfortable and feminine than its Georgian predecessor. A flower-painted carpet partially covers the 'stencilled' floor, which is made of patterned card to simulate a simple design. Flowers, writing equipment and upholstered seating add to the homely effect.*

RIGHT *Rich colours and fabrics can be used in the Biedermeier room. White satin-stripe paper is a regular wallpaper sample and the patterned ribbon edged with gold thread will give a rich effect when used as a border.*

HOW TO MAKE AND DRAPE CURTAINS

Curtains in heavy materials were arranged in elaborate swathes. Double-sided velvet ribbon is a good choice for a rectangular or square window, as some of the fabric will be visible from outside the dolls' house.

Windows with a rounded top are more difficult to curtain. The simplest method is to cut a card base to surround the window. Drape and fix the curtains to the card, which can be lightly glued to the wall complete with curtains and tie-backs.

1 Cut a card pattern ½in (12mm) wide to fit around the window and continue it down to floor level.

2 Cut two pieces of ribbon or fabric, each long enough to reach from the centre top of the card, across and down to the bottom, plus one-third as long again to allow for draping.

3 Start at the centre top. Fix one end of the ribbon with double-sided Scotch tape and drape to make a pleasing shape, fixing with tape at strategic points – this will allow you to make adjustments as you continue. Now repeat for the other side, checking that the two sides are symmetrical.

4 Use thin cord, gold or coloured, to make tie-backs. These can be fixed to the back of the curtains and also to the card base in order to keep them in place.

5 Make a pelmet which will cover the join at the top. Drape and fix in the same way and finish with a cord tie or bow to match the tie-backs.

6 Try the arrangement at the window using Blu-tack as a temporary fixing while you check the length. There is no need to hem, because this would add excessive bulk. Cut to length with sharp scissors and use a wooden cocktail stick to run a thin trail of all-purpose glue along the lower end to prevent fraying.

7 Finally, attach to the wall around the window with double-sided tape.

Centre top

Add tiebacks →

← Add tiebacks

Sill

Floor level

FRENCH STYLE

French decorations and furniture have a charm all their own. A French dolls' house interior, whether it is based on the simple country look or on the grand rooms of a château, will certainly give an impression very different from an English dolls' house. French taste is conservative and thrifty: furniture is often kept for generations and fabric patterns are repeated. Nothing changes!

A country room can be sparsely furnished but still be full of atmosphere. Tiled floors in halls and downstairs parlours are almost universal, while the installation of a woodburning stove instead of a fireplace is an option. A plain wooden settle rather than upholstered armchairs, and a pretty cabinet to fill with china, can be bought from mass-produced ranges of dolls' house furniture.

A small French bedroom may have bare floorboards and pine furniture. There is usually a tall wardrobe or armoire, and an old-fashioned washstand substitutes for the lack of a bathroom. Bedsteads are commonly of brass or pine, with both head and footboards.

The entrance hall in a seventeenth-century French château (see page 52) again illustrates the difference in styles between French and English or American interiors. The furniture would be contemporary with the English William and Mary hall featured on page 37, but whereas the English version may well have been refurnished and redecorated, the French hall would probably still look much the same today.

LEFT *The Continental stove and elegant china cabinet typify French provincial style.*

ABOVE *This room has been designed as the home of an artist. Art materials scattered on the pine table and a painting on the easel clearly set the scene.*

LEFT *The bed is not made up but is instead used to lay out a fine embroidered waistcoat. There are no ornaments or clutter, and the pine furniture is plain, but this fresh-looking bedroom conveys the essence of French style.*

ABOVE *The hall is elegant without being ostentatious. You need only a few pieces of furniture to achieve a similar look of discreet grandeur. The armoire, table and corner cupboard are ready-made, exact copies of the real thing painted in a traditional colour. The impressive flooring is giftwrap in bronze and gold chequered squares. A bust of Napoleon in a corner is evidence of the republican sympathies of the house owner.*

IDEAS FOR A FRENCH ENTRANCE HALL

● Add a bust of Napoleon: the one pictured above was coloured by a professional painter of military models, but you can buy one to paint yourself.

● Choose suitable French paintings to frame with gilt picture-frame mouldings. Landscapes such as the one used in this room (painted by Claude Lorrain in the late seventeenth century) are ideal and can be found in art gallery catalogues and listings.

● Paint a longcase clock. Strip and repaint an inexpensive imported model with a distressed finish to resemble an old inherited piece. Instructions are given on page 140.

● Arrange flowers in a trailing arrangement to stand on a pedestal: a formal arrangement will look best in this type of room.

● Repaint a cheap metal bust or statue to simulate bronze. Instructions are given on page 142.

RIGHT *An urn on a marbled pedestal shows off an arrangement by a professional miniaturist.*

VICTORIAN

The Victorian period is a favourite with dolls' house enthusiasts, whether they are concerned primarily with collecting or, instead, prefer to make their own accessories. In the early part of Queen Victoria's reign rooms were relatively restrained, but by the mid-nineteenth century clutter abounded: part of the enjoyment can be to see how many miniatures you can fit into a room.

In the 1870s the growing influence of William Morris heralded new ideas in interior decoration in Britain, including white paintwork, naturalistic floral curtains instead of heavy velvet drapes, and painted furniture. This was a gradual but vast change from the dark and rich decor of mid-Victorian rooms.

Tartan carpets used by Queen Victoria and Prince Albert in their private rooms at Balmoral were soon copied, and these can be provided by using plaid woollen dress material or a wool-and-cotton mixture (see pages 54-55 and 75). Lace curtains were still used, often combined with outer curtains made from William Morris fabrics.

Victorian chairs were well-upholstered and made in interesting shapes, some of them reproduced from older examples. Balloon-back chairs are still popular today, while the prie-dieu (a chair designed for kneeling on rather than sitting) has gone out of fashion.

Arranging a room which shows new ideas being incorporated offers a great opportunity for the miniaturist, who can decide what to put in and what might be too forward-looking to include.

ABOVE *This luxurious High Victorian room is the setting for Christmas festivities.*

ABOVE *This comfortable parlour in a Scottish Borders castle is an example of the time when High Victorian was beginning to give way to newer styles. Home and the family were very important and family activities are catered for: a fitted workbox is open ready for use, and a violin, a canterbury (to hold sheet music), a newspaper and some refreshments are all provided.*

The 'stone' walls of the Scottish Borders castle room pictured here are rendered with plaster in a pinkish tone, simulated by a plain dolls' house wallpaper, although emulsion paint would give a similar effect. In an ordinary house of the time rather than a castle room, a William Morris miniaturized wallpaper might be preferable: many patterns are available. The Victorians were not afraid to mix patterns together, and even if you choose wallpaper it would still be appropriate to use patterned curtains.

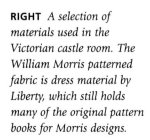

RIGHT *A selection of materials used in the Victorian castle room. The William Morris patterned fabric is dress material by Liberty, which still holds many of the original pattern books for Morris designs.*

PROJECT

HOW TO MAKE A DOOR

ABOVE *A massive oak door suits the castle room, and is surrounded by copies of oil paintings by Rossetti and Waterhouse. A Davenport desk in the corner of the room has an account book on top, ready to write up the household expenditure. Because they were small and contained many useful drawers these desks were especially favoured by women.*

The Arts and Crafts movement was in full swing by the end of the nineteenth century, and plain oak doors with handwrought iron handles were favoured. A double (non-opening) door suits this room but it can be scaled down to a single door with a handle on one side for a smaller room.

To make the double door, use ½in (12mm) wide stripwood, with a slightly wider piece for the lintel. The door frame shown is made from a shaped wood moulding with the thicker edge on the outside edge, but plain stripwood could be used.

The doorstep is a block of wood ¾in (20mm) wide and ⅜in (10mm) deep.

1 Decide on the height and width of the door including the frame. Cut a piece of card to this size and trim off ⅛in (3mm) all round so that the card edges will not show when the wood is fitted on top.

2 Cut four pieces of stripwood to the right length and glue to the card base. Add the side frame pieces next and lastly the lintel across the top.

3 Arts and Crafts style handles are not easy to find. For a good simulation, glue on two metal plate stands. As the part of the metal to be glued on is very tiny, use superglue which bonds metal to wood instantly. To avoid sticking your fingers to the door or handle, lay the door flat and use tweezers to pick up and hold the handle while you squeeze on a very little glue; then press the handle firmly in place.

4 Cut the doorstep approximately 1in (25mm) wider than the completed door and fix it to the wall. Either glue on the complete door and frame above the step, or attach it with double-sided Scotch tape.

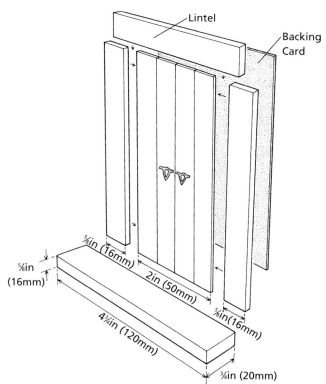

Lintel

Backing Card

⅝in (16mm)

⅝in (16mm)

2in (50mm)

⅝in (16mm)

4¾in (120mm)

¾in (20mm)

HOW TO MAKE THE FIREPLACE

You can buy a 'stone' fireplace made in cast resin, or you can easily make a 'granite' one from oddments of wood left over from other work. You will need several different thicknesses of wood strip. The fireplace shown measures 3¾in (95mm) wide and 3⅝in (92mm) high, plus a mantelshelf. Measurements, of course, can be varied to suit the size of the room.

1 Cut three pieces of ⅜in (10mm) square dowelling, one 3½in (90mm) long for the top and two 3¼in (82mm) long for the sides. Glue them together.

RIGHT *The completed fireplace in the room. The mantelshelf displays a dried flower arrangement in a glass dome. 'The Monarch of the Glen' by Sir Edwin Landseer hangs above. The fire is laid with scrunched-up newspaper and slivers of matchsticks as kindling, as though ready to light.*

PROJECT

2 Cut two pieces of ⅜in (10mm) right-angled stripwood each 3⅞in (98mm) long and glue them to the outsides of the side pieces of the basic shape.

3 Mark the centre and glue the mantelshelf on top, checking that it extends equally on either side.

4 To simulate granite, paint the fireplace with mid-grey matt model enamel and streak and smudge with a darker grey. Only a few markings are needed.

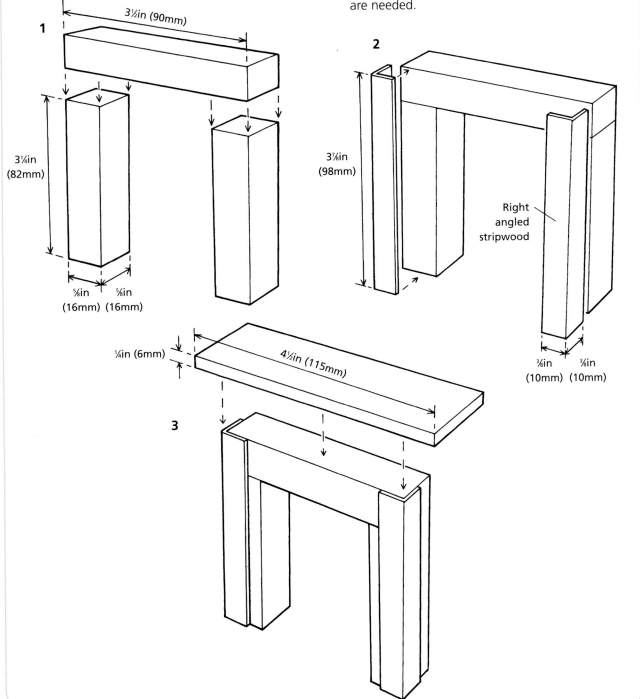

1

3½in (90mm)

3¼in (82mm)

⅝in (16mm)   ⅝in (16mm)

2

3⅞in (98mm)

Right angled stripwood

⅜in (10mm)   ⅜in (10mm)

¼in (6mm)

4½in (115mm)

3

HOW TO MAKE CURTAINS

Use William Morris dress fabric to make curtains. If part will be seen from outside the windows, the curtains should be double-sided and hemmed.

1 Cut the fabric double the width that is required for each finished curtain plus ¾in (20mm) extra to allow for two ⅜in (10mm) turnings at the side join.

2 Cut each piece to the required length plus ⅜in (10mm) for the bottom hem.

3 Fold in half lengthwise and press.

4 Turn in ⅜in (10mm) on either side and at the bottom and press. Slipstitch neatly together.

5 Gather the top edges together and firmly finish off the thread.

6 Attach to the walls on each side of the window with double-sided tape.

Make a pelmet, doubling the fabric in the same way but making the fold across the bottom and hemming at the top edge. To fit well over the gathered tops of the curtains, the pelmet should be made ½in (12mm) wider than the measurement of the two finished curtains when it is attached around the window.

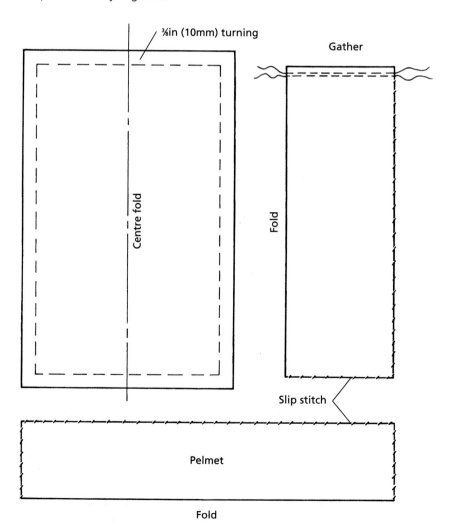

ACCESSORIES

A Victorian room is the ideal setting in which to show off your own work if you enjoy miniature embroidery or needlepoint.

● Domed bases can be purchased for footstools, with removable padded tops to cover with your own designs.

● Firescreens are another option: choose one where the frame can be taken apart to set in your own work.

● Make plenty of cushions. To make them squashy and comfortable-looking do not overstuff: the smallest wisp of synthetic wadding is sufficient. Avoid cotton wool as filling, because it will look and feel lumpy.

● Needlepoint and crossstitch bellpulls and carpets will fit in well. Charts and complete kits including silk or wool thread are widely available, or you can scale down a simple full-size design by leaving out much of the fine detail and working on a small-size canvas.

● Glass domes with removable bases are inexpensive and can be used to show off an arrangement of dried flowers or tiny shells. Make a base with Blu-tack and start with a twig in the centre. Build up an arrangement, gluing on flowers or shells with impact glue, checking now and again that the 'tree' is not too wide for the glass dome to fit over it. To avoid glue on fingers, dab on the glue with a cocktail stick and use tweezers to fix on the flowers or the shells.

WARNING

Impact glue (superglue) must be treated with caution. If you do get some on your finger, wash in warm water immediately, or it will dry leaving a sticky residue which will take time to wear off.

LEFT *A needlepoint bell pull worked from a kit can be used in a drawing room or bedroom.*

ABOVE *A well-filled Victorian nursery has great appeal to the collector of miniature toys.*

THE ARTS AND CRAFTS MOVEMENT

By the turn of the century the influence of the Arts and Crafts movement was felt in the average home. The simplicity and hand-made look of the new designs for furniture, the appeal of beaten copper and pewter, realistic paintings of contemporary life, and tapestries based on medieval originals gradually increased in popularity.

Liberty's store in London had opened in 1875, and it enthusiastically promoted the new trends. People went to exhibitions of handicrafts, and many husbands took up carpentry as a hobby and made simple tables and stools, while others tried metal-work. It was a time for learning new skills which could be used to beautify the home.

RIGHT *A plain, sturdy chair made in oak with a drop-in leather seat. Good workmanship and strong construction followed the country chairmaker's tradition.*

ABOVE *This Arts and Crafts room is the work of the members of a dolls' house club. The attention to detail catches the mood of the period, and the style of the room box itself complements the contents.*

ABOVE *The billiard table and lighting are the centrepiece of this room which was made by a dolls' house group. It contains elements from two English houses which are open to view: Standen in West Sussex and Wightwick Manor in the West Midlands.*

In large country houses of the kind once owned by industrial magnates, a billiard room was obligatory. In England, billiard rooms can be viewed in several houses now owned by the National Trust, and these provide a rich source of inspiration for miniaturists.

IDEAS FOR ARTS AND CRAFTS ROOMS

● Plain wooden floors with a rug or small carpet were considered hygienic.

● Tiles can be used to surround a plain wooden fireplace, either in ceramic or pictured on card or paper.

● Curtains should show the pervasive William Morris influence: Liberty dress fabrics are miniature versions of the original curtain and upholstery fabrics. Net curtains were no longer in favour.

LEFT *The sinuous lines of Art Nouveau were still popular: silver and pewter jugs in Liberty style looked well on new furniture. The revolving bookcase was first made in 1890, and updated designs continued until the 1950s. The one shown here is a version from the 1920s.*

LEFT *The fireplace has a surround of handpainted tiles and a display of blue-and-white porcelain on the mantelshelf, which is in the taste of Victorian artistic interiors. The well-finished woodwork in this room is especially noteworthy: the plain panelling refers back to medieval style.*

● In country houses, candles and oil lamps were still used, but in towns gas mantles were installed. There are some pretty miniature versions available.

● Bathrooms were still not in general use. A bedroom can have a washstand complete with toilet set of ewer, basin and soap dish, like the earlier Victorian version, but by this time they might be backed with a curtain rather than tiles.

LEFT *Built-in seating on either side of a fireplace developed from the idea of a Tudor settle and became known as a 'cosy corner'. It was featured strongly in early catalogues from the London furniture store, Heal's. Put a high-backed settle near to the fireplace to convey this effect. The miniature shown is made in boxwood.*

ABOVE *A replica of Pierre le Faguay's Archer statuette shows the continental art nouveau influence. This accurately detailed model is cast in pewter and painted to resemble the original bronze and ivory.*

MODERN LIVING

The 1950s were the beginning of a great change in interior decoration. In Britain, during the years of austerity which followed the Second World War, people were starved of colour and ready to try something new and adventurous.

Fabrics and wallpapers in up-to-the-minute patterns began to appear, and they were used in rooms still furnished with a mixture of traditional pieces and objects passed on by relatives. New furniture designs provided another huge style change and these were incorporated into existing room schemes. The resulting mélange may have looked a little incongruous but it was certainly different.

ABOVE *These chairs follow early influences. It is difficult to credit that the originals, which were signed and dated by the maker, were made in 1951 at roughly the same time as the new moulded plastic furniture shown on page 64.*

ABOVE *This cheerful room would have been very up-to-date for its time, with a brightly coloured fitted carpet and contrasting wallpapers – on the fireplace wall a dolls' house miniature stripe, and on the others an art paper from a stationers. It became the fashion to emphasize one wall in this way. The 1950s furniture includes a lounging chair, which can be reclined, and a 'wireless' set.*

ABOVE *A reclining chair, workbox and side table with castors from the 1950s.*

ABOVE *Moulded plastic furniture was an alternative to more traditional pieces. It was light, cheerful and easy to keep clean, and it became an instant success. This set of dining table and chairs is typical of the new designs.*

HOW TO MAKE A 1950S-STYLE FIREPLACE

To make the fireplace you will need a piece of balsa or foamboard approximately ½in (12mm) thick, 4½in (115mm) long and 3½in (90mm) high, some plain shiny card and oddments of wood.

1 Cut the balsa to size and mark the centre. Cut an opening approximately 1½in (40mm) wide and 1¾in (45mm) high as shown.

2 Cut a piece of card slightly larger than the balsa and glue it on to the wooden base. Trim the edges to fit, and cut out the opening with a craft knife.

3 Make the hearth from a piece of ¼in (6mm) thick wood or card, approximately 1¼in (30mm) deep and 6in (150mm) long. Cover with card to match the fireplace, folding over the front edge and underneath. Glue firmly. There is no need to cover the ends of the hearth unless the fireplace is to be fitted at the side of a room where the ends may be seen.

4 Add a wooden mantelshelf, stained medium oak. This should be only marginally longer than the width of the fireplace.

You might want to put a miniature electric fire in the opening instead of a grate, to add to the 1950s feeling.

ABOVE *The 1930s pre-war fireplace was soon replaced by something sleeker. This simple fireplace is typical of 1950s style and is easy to miniaturize.*

IDEAS FOR THE 1950S ROOM

● Curtains should be to the sill or just a little below. (As fabric was still in short supply, floor-length curtains were not an option.) Use a floral or brightly-coloured geometric patterned fabric.

● Make plain skirting boards from ½in (12mm) stripwood, stained medium oak or painted cream or white.

● Use felt to provide a plain fitted carpet. This is authentic, as wool was not available and very thick felt was sometimes used as a carpet substitute.

● Make a low coffee table. Use a small box as a base and paint it matt black. Top with shiny patterned card glued on to a piece of wood to simulate patterned Formica, which was generally favoured because it was very easy to wipe clean.

● Coffee had become the fashionable drink, and almost eclipsed tea as the nation's favourite beverage. Use a decorative fridge magnet as a coffee machine.

● Pictures should be bright and cheerful but not abstract.

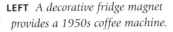

● Leave some knitting lying around: it was a popular hobby in the 1950s. Knit a few rows on darning needles with one strand of thin tapestry wool. Transfer the knitting to long pins (preferably with coloured heads), leaving a long end of wool to wind into a ball. Fix the ball with a dab of glue to prevent it from unravelling.

LEFT *A decorative fridge magnet provides a 1950s coffee machine.*

CONTEMPORARY STYLES

Today's rooms are interesting to design and complete. Many hobbyists like to arrange a room or even a complete dolls' house based on their own home, and to track down miniature versions of fabrics and floor coverings similar to their full-size counterparts. There should be no problem in finding 1/12 versions of modern furniture which, if not exactly the same, will be a good approximation to your own.

Modern styles allow free rein to the imagination: you can achieve spectacular decorative effects by using paper and card rather than expensive materials. I have designed two ultra-modern rooms which are adaptable and could be given a very different look with your own choice of colour scheme.

Colour is the key to the dramatic effect of my international-style room. The walls are painted plain cream as a neutral background for the hangings and to provide a contrast with the floor covering, a wallpaper sample in a vibrant orange-red with touches of gold. The feature fireplace is a gift box cut in half. The remaining half can be painted to give a different look in another room.

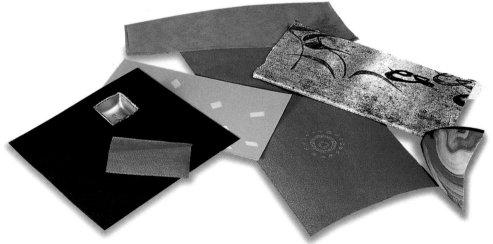

ABOVE *This is the sort of room you might find today in a superior apartment or an expensive hotel. The woven carpet hanging over the fireplace is a 1/12 design from Turkey. The hanging on the side wall is a mosaic tile picture which has been cut from a magazine.*

LEFT *Choose paper and card in vivid colours for a contemporary look.*

HOW TO MAKE A TABLE

A low round table is effective and easy to make. For the base, use a plastic top from a jar about 2¼-2½in (55mm-65mm) in diameter. One from a jar of instant coffee may be just right for the purpose, and you may even find that it suits your colour scheme. If not, plastic can be painted.

1 Cut a circle of thin card or wood ¼in (6mm) thick and approximately 3in (75mm) in diameter to make the table top.

HINT

Small perspex boxes used to pack jewellery (and sometimes dolls' house miniatures) can be used just as they are as tables, and will look good in a modern room. One ornament or vase of flowers displayed on top will make a bold statement.

2 Draw round a cup or glass to mark a circle accurately before you cut.

3 Paint the edge and a border round both top and underneath.

4 Cut a circle of marbled card slightly smaller than the table top and glue on to leave a narrow painted border.

5 Glue the completed top to the base or fix it in place with double-sided Scotch tape.

ABOVE *Plain modern glass on a marble-topped table makes an attractive centrepiece for the room.*

SOFAS

In modern rooms sofas are more in evidence than armchairs, and may be covered in synthetic materials or leather rather than in traditional fabrics.

One useful covering for the miniaturist to use is plasticized paper flower-wrap. This has a faint self-pattern and a slight sheen, which gives it a lovely appearance: it has, of course, the added attraction of being provided completely free whenever you buy a bunch of flowers. It is strong and will look like fabric when the sofa is finished.

When using paper flowerwrap as a covering you can build up as many layers as you need so that no edges of the polystyrene base show through. Two or more layers may be necessary. (*See diagram and key for each section.*)

To finish the room, keep ornaments to a minimum: one or two striking pieces (mineral samples, for example) will look superb.

PROJECT

HOW TO MAKE A SOFA WITH ARMS

(This sofa is shown in the room setting on page 66)

1 Start with a small expanded polystyrene box approximately 3½in (90mm) long by 3½in (90mm) wide and 1½ in (40mm) deep. These are used to pack electrical equipment and parts. As they are designed as protective packaging, the sides of the box will be around ½in (12mm) thick, ideal to form the sides and back of a 1/12 sofa.

2 Cut the box in half to make a matching pair.

3 Cut paper patterns for each section of the sofa (see diagrams), allowing extra to fold underneath to finish off. The pieces should also be cut marginally wider than the sections to be covered and trimmed after fixing in place, using double-sided tape rather than glue.

To cover the base:

4 Fix on a piece of paper which has been cut to fit inside each arm.

5 Fix a strip of paper to the outside of one arm, continuing along the back to finish at the front of the second arm.

6 Cut a strip to fit over front and top of each arm, folding under at the front edge to fix underneath and finishing at the back of the arm.

7 Cut and fix on a piece of paper to cover over the back and seat, again folding under at the base of both front and back to finish underneath the sofa.

8 Using sharp scissors, trim excess flowerwrap neatly from joins.

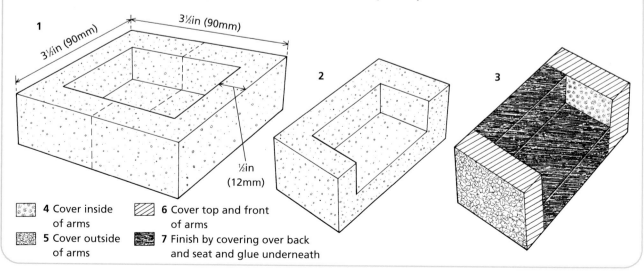

1   3½in (90mm)   3½in (90mm)   ½in (12mm)

2

3

4 Cover inside of arms
5 Cover outside of arms
6 Cover top and front of arms
7 Finish by covering over back and seat and glue underneath

PROJECT

HOW TO MAKE A SOFA WITHOUT ARMS

If you are unable to find a box to form the base of the sofa, you can make a simple armless sofa which will fit well into a modern room. A suitable size is 3½in (90mm) long, 1½in (40mm) deep and approximately 2⅜in (60mm) high, but dimensions can be varied.

1 Use corrugated card packaging to make the base. Fold it over several times to make a thickness of approximately ⅝in (16mm), then tape it together securely. Make the back and seat cushions from the same packaging (that from a chocolate box will be especially suitable as it is slightly squashy). The back should be folded about ⅜in (10mm) thick and the seat and back cushions about ¼in (6mm) thick.

2 Cover the sofa with flower-wrap. First cut a strip of paper to fold over from end to end of the base and fix it in place with double-sided tape as before. Then cut and fold another strip of paper to fold over the base from front to back, over the first strip, and fix it underneath.

3 Cover the back, seat cushion and two smaller cushions in the same way.

4 Cut a piece of plain card to make a support for the back. Fold it in half and fix to the base back and underneath. Cover with flower-wrap. Fix the back and seat cushions in place, then add the two small back cushions.

ABOVE *Red cushions made from non-fray seam binding complete the sofa.*

SAFETY NOTE

Expanded polystyrene is easy to cut but liable to crumble. Use a craft knife. Start by digging the point in and then cut carefully. Remember that it will be impossible to cut yourself if you make sure that you always cut away from your other hand. LOOK BEFORE YOU CUT.

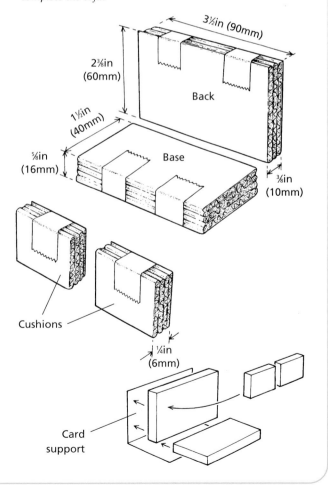

A MODERN CHINESE ROOM

Exploring decorative styles from a different culture is a learning process which will allow you plenty of invention. Again, the effect can be achieved at minimum expense with paper, card and, this time, the inclusion of oriental artefacts.

For the wall covering, try using bronze-gold art paper pierced with random holes over a plain, light-coloured card to emphasize the effect of the overlay. Art paper of this kind is fragile, and the best way to attach it to the card base is to fix double-sided Scotch tape to the card along all edges, and then press the paper in place to avoid tearing it. It is essential to line up the top and side edges carefully. Finally fix the paper-covered card to the room wall.

The fireplace is designed to suit the oriental style of the room. Make it in the same way as the one in the 1950s room, but add a wider mantelshelf to extend about ½in (12mm) on either side. Cover the mantelshelf with a grey-green shiny paper so that it resembles soapstone.

ABOVE *Tortoiseshell patterned card makes an interesting door. A black mapping pin is used as a door handle.*

Make non-opening doors from wood or card. One possibility is to cut a patterned card from a stationery file (as shown above). Door surrounds can be made by using the border from around a Chinese postcard, mounted on thin stripwood.

ABOVE *This room is in striking contrast to the international-style room shown earlier. The floor covering is a silk-finish picture-mounting board. The bamboo in the vase is real, but this will not last: use pieces from a rattan tablemat for a similar effect. A laughing Chinese Buddha sits in the fireplace instead of a grate.*

HOW TO MAKE A 'BAMBOO' TABLE

1 Use a small corrugated card box for the base of the table. Alternatively, make your own 'box' by folding and gluing corrugated card together to form a box about 2½in (65mm) square.

2 Paint with black satin-finish model enamel.

3 When dry, use a gold marker pen to add small lines to resemble bamboo.

4 Cut a table top slightly larger than your box from thin wood. Cut and glue on a picture of lacquer: the one shown was part of a postcard depicting a lacquer tray, and the borders were used for the door surround shown in the two photographs on the facing page.

LEFT *Corrugated card forms the base for this 'bamboo' table, which is as firm and strong as wood.*

ECONOMICAL IDEAS FOR A CHINESE ROOM

● Fat, jolly Chinese buddhas are available from gift shops at minimal cost.

● A more expensive figure of pale-coloured resin, like the one on the mantelshelf, will look like jade.

● Make low seats from wood or foamboard covered with red shiny paper.

● Paint wooden bowls to resemble lacquer. Paint the outsides with satin-finish black model enamel.

As soon as they are dry, colour the insides of the bowls with a gold marker pen of the sort which needs to be shaken before and during use. The gold will be more realistic than metallic paint.

● A free alternative to wooden bowls is to use acorn cups if you are able to find any.

HINT

Most card, including postcards, has a visible thin white edge. It is essential to colour all edges to avoid spoiling the effect of your completed miniature with a white streak. Use a black marker pen or calligraphy pen on the edges of the card chosen for the door surround and table top. If you use coloured card, the edges can be tinted to match with a felt-tip pen or crayon in the closest shade you have.

BELOW *A lacquer effect can be achieved using model enamel and a gold marker pen.*

Service rooms

KITCHENS

Period kitchens in dolls' houses can feature not only food, but replicas of gadgets which are no longer in use, such as a butter churn, a table mincer or a flat iron. We may decide upon a replica of our mother's or grandmother's kitchen as we remember it from childhood. Going even further back in time, there are now kitchen museums where we can see how the Tudor, Georgian or Victorian kitchen was arranged.

Replicas of much of the equipment in both period and modern kitchens are made in 1/12. Victorian kitchens staffed by servants contained a huge array of gadgets, while in more modest homes cook managed with only basic cooking tools.

Modern kitchens look delightful reproduced in miniature, because it is always fascinating to see the equipment we use every day in a tiny size.

RIGHT *Mrs Beeton would have approved of this neatly arranged kitchen with its well-filled store cupboard and general air of cleanliness.*

ABOVE *In contrast to the kitchen shown on the facing page, this Edinburgh tenement kitchen of 1899 contains the sort of basic equipment which the average housewife would have used. The Arts and Crafts movement was well under way by this time, but the new ideas had not yet percolated through to all levels of society.*

LEFT *Compare this French kitchen with its Scottish counterpart of much the same date. Both rooms are small, but the French version has a more airy and uncluttered feeling. It features a white continental stove rather than a black cast iron range: doubtless the French housewife has space to hang washing outdoors.*

ABOVE *Made in Japan, this unusual miniature is a Japanese rice steamer: a self-contained kitchen.*

ABOVE *Kitchen units from a wide range of styles for the modern dolls' house: this design is made in light-coloured wood with mahogany inlay and a replica laminated worktop. The ceramic hob, cooker with glass-panelled door and white sink are the basic appliances which can be supplemented with built-in dishwasher, refrigerator and freezer.*

LEFT *An inexpensive fridge magnet which can be used in the dolls' house kitchen – complete with toast.*

ABOVE *An up-market modern kitchen designed by a maker who enjoys tackling anything from medieval style to ultra-modern. The spotlights in the ceiling are an unusual feature in a dolls' house room.*

BATHROOMS

Bathrooms are a relatively modern innovation, as frequent washing was not thought of as essential until fairly recently. Proper bathrooms were a late Victorian idea, and even then they were rare. It was common for a huge house to have a single bathroom: everyone except the house owners had to make do with a bowl and jugs of water. This continued until after the First World War and into the 1920s.

Dolls' houses also tend to be somewhat short on bathrooms, because when you have few rooms to arrange the bathroom is often the one to be left out. If you can find the space you will enjoy designing and decorating one to suit your house – and it is guaranteed to attract attention. A water closet with a chain which can be pulled seems to fascinate young and old alike, and one assembled from a kit might suit a not-too-modern bathroom.

In the country house the bathroom has never been the most comfortable of rooms. Until the 1930s plumbing was fairly primitive, and even then hot water was provided by a dangerous-looking gas geyser over the bath.

There were occasional exceptions to drab, unheated bathrooms. In some Edwardian stately homes, lavish marble bathrooms had a free-standing bath, usually in the centre of the room, although this still had to be filled (and emptied) by relays of servants using buckets and jugs.

There would be a fire lit in the grate during cold weather, as the bathroom was usually adapted from a former bedroom with a fireplace. More workaday bathrooms were furnished with unwanted chairs and tables from other rooms in the house, in a mixture of period styles.

We all have our own idea of the perfect bathroom. A period dolls' house can manage with a washstand in a bedroom, but a modern home is incomplete without a bath or shower room, however small.

LEFT *A marble-topped washstand with tiled back was customary in most country house bedrooms in the early part of the twentieth century. The pretty porcelain toilet set of ewer and basin has a matching soapdish with perforated top for water to drain.*

ABOVE *A marbled bathroom which might have belonged to someone very wealthy. The bath sits on a raised marble panel and the towel is monogrammed. The interesting shower was invented during the Regency period and has been included in this bathroom for good measure: it probably belonged to an ancestor before the bath was installed.*

HINT

Use thin marbled card instead of wallpaper to marble a bathroom. As a centrepiece, try adding a pictured marble panel so that the bath is raised up as the central feature. Using white tape, monogram a towel fringed at each end, and write the initials in fineline black pen or ballpoint.

ABOVE *A stylish bath with shower handset for the modern bathroom. 'Glass' shelves on the wall or a bathroom cabinet could be added to show off toiletries and mini toothbrushes.*

DISPLAY
A SPECIAL
COLLECTION

3

ABOVE *Some special collections can be housed effectively in either a formal or an informal setting. These handpainted pewter rabbits can be arranged on a nursery windowsill or in a shop. As the collection grows it will need a larger display area.*

CHINA AND PORCELAIN

Many hobbyists own at least one dolls' house where miniatures are arranged in period or modern rooms. After that first house, some collectors will decide to specialize in one type of miniature which especially appeals to them, whether it be paintings, porcelains or woodturnings.

To display a collection of this kind, a shop, gallery or specially-designated room may sometimes provide a more suitable background than a dolls' house which is already furnished. A collection of similar objects grouped together always looks more impressive than one scattered around.

In the eighteenth century a large country house often had a china room, both to store and to show off attractive porcelain. This idea can be copied by the collector of miniatures. Walls can be used to show off sets of plates, so that even an extensive collection will fit into a small room. Larger pieces can be arranged on tables.

LEFT *Japanese Kakiemonware porcelain is a collectors' item whether in full size or miniature scale. The original is a rarity which was made only for a short time at the end of the seventeenth century. These lidded jars, bottles and tea bowl are handthrown and painted with delicate flowers to give an almost translucent effect.*

ABOVE *This room is part of an antiques shop where the colour scheme and Delft-tiled fireplace were planned to complement the mainly blue-and-white china. The collection includes a bone china two-handled mug which commemorates Prince William's christening.*

HINT

Plan a symmetrical arrangement of plates and attach them to the wall with Blu-tack, which will make it easy to move them around until you are satisfied with the effect.

WOODTURNINGS AND WOODEN OBJECTS

Wood is another attractive material. It is not cold to the touch like stone or marble; it feels good and often smells good; and the available range of colour and texture is immense. It isn't surprising that many collectors relish the variety of small objects which are a product of the woodturner's skill and imagination.

BELOW *Woodturned items on tables form part of a shop display. In the dolls' house kitchen or dining room many of these bowls and jars could be arranged as though ready for use rather than piled up for sale.*

LEFT *People who enjoy wood and its uses need not limit themselves to turnings. This busy toymaker's workshop shows off wood in a different way.*

ARMOUR

Armour fascinates hobbyists who are interested in the history of warfare or the age of chivalry. There are many distinctive types, so that it is possible to form a varied collection. Some of them are made by miniaturists working in the dolls' house field, but many museum and gift shops also stock suits of armour, helmets and weapons based on historical examples and intended as souvenirs: these too, are usually in 1/12 scale.

Even at this size a suit of armour can be quite heavy, because these miniatures are usually made of pewter. It is best to provide a firm base so that the armour cannot fall over and damage small objects nearby. A really large piece of Blu-tack will solve the problem, giving added security even when a base is provided. One suit of armour in a hallway can be the start of an interesting collection.

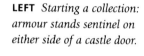
LEFT *Starting a collection: armour stands sentinel on either side of a castle door.*

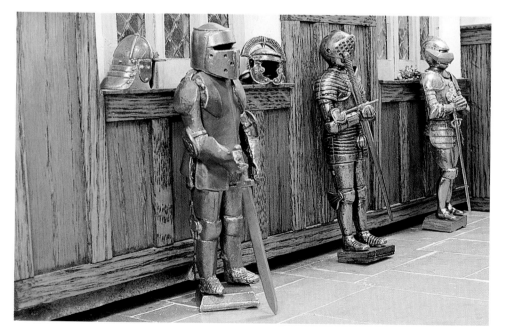

LEFT *Suits of armour are impressive standing in an oak panelled corridor. From left to right: handmade pewter armour which has been finished to give an impression of age; a representation of King Henry VIII's armour; and a suit of sixteenth-century gilded French armour. The vizors can be raised and lowered. On the windowsill, a Cromwellian lobstertail helmet and a Roman helmet complete the array.*

MUSICAL INSTRUMENTS

Musical instruments are one speciality which can be arranged singly or in small groups in almost any room. A music room, such as the Regency example shown on page 43, can be included in a dolls' house as long as the instruments are of the corresponding period.

ABOVE *A handmade cello with fine stringing. The instrument is French polished, which gives a soft sheen to the wood. Here it is shown next to a Regency chair, but a cello could be included in a modern room, too.*

BELOW *A single manual harpsichord based on an original made by Jacob Kirckman in the mid-eighteenth century. The miniature incorporates burr walnut, boxwood, walnut, amboyna and tulipwood. Fittings are of brass, and there are three sets of strings. The needlepoint cover on the music stool is worked in Florentine stitch, popularly known as flamestitch. Early period instruments will be of special interest to anyone who enjoys ancient music.*

One problem with slender wind instruments is how to fix them to prevent them rolling away. A tiny blob of Blu-tack or a thin strip of double-sided tape are two solutions. Take care when fixing them to a table or wall surface, because if pressure is applied too strongly at one point, the wood may snap.

ABOVE *A collection of period instruments is shown off on an oak table in the minstrels' gallery of a Tudor house. They include treble and bass recorders, a shawm, a lute and a psaltery.*

RIGHT *Wind instruments displayed on a wall in a Tudor room. In the foreground, a lute is propped against an oak stool, ready for playing.*

ART

One advantage of displaying paintings in a gallery is that you can rearrange the artworks from time to time without upsetting the balance of a furnished room.

Compare the symmetrical hanging of the paintings in this classical gallery with the informal arrangement of pictures in the Victorian castle room on pages 54-55. It may help you to decide which type of background you prefer. Emphasize the hanging space by providing an additional 'frame' to surround the pictures. A silk cord fixed below the cornice with tasselled ends hanging on either side will add a touch of elegance in a gallery devoted to classical art. Add a few 'art objects' so that the floor is not entirely bare.

A simple, inexpensive way in which to acquire a comprehensive art collection is to use small pictures cut from exhibition catalogues or from home and decoration magazines which have art listings. It is essential that the pictures are printed with colours in register on good quality paper, and that you choose the correct type of framing for the period.

ABOVE *Classical art is shown in a small gallery in a Georgian house. The room decorations are also in Georgian style, with a dado rail above marbled walls, a chequered tile floor and a magnificent stone fireplace which is based on a design by William Kent and simulated in cast resin. Colours are kept pale so that the paintings show up well.*

A gallery which is devoted to modern art should, to my mind, have plain white walls. It can show a series of changing exhibitions, kept up to date with paintings taken from the latest listings and cata-logues. It may be unnecessary to frame modern abstract paintings: again, they often look best mounted on white card, which will also provide a border.

ABOVE *Pictures in course of arrangement and the addition of some unusual modern sculpture give a lively feeling to this gallery. The sculptures, fashioned from gold wire and beads originally intended for jewellery-making, were assembled in minutes.*

ABOVE *Gilded picture frame moulding is best for period art. A wide, heavy frame will complement an early landscape, while more delicate seascapes such as the small Turners will benefit from plainer frames, perhaps with simple beading.*

ABOVE *This exhibition has a more tranquil atmosphere: the pictures are calmer, and the tall metal 'sculptures' (from a gallery shop) were designed to hold postcards. They can also be used as a modern alternative to an easel.*

LEFT *What better subject for display than this 'swagger' painting by John Singer Sargent, who specialized in flattering his sitters? To emphasize its importance, the painting is framed in an impressive gilt moulding.*

My gallery is in a room box measuring 15in (380mm) wide, 8in (200mm) deep and 11in (280mm) high. The floor and ceiling are interchangeable, so that the gallery can be used either way up. In the first version the floor is made of thick, silvery paper with a modernist design, while in the second the floor is of black paper with a raised effect similar to bubblewrap. Either is suitable for floor or ceiling.

ABOVE *These frames have been chosen with care. The Rossetti oil should have a gilded surround. Japanese prints are framed traditionally in thin black moulding, while the Miró looks best in a plain wooden frame.*

FRAMING

Before framing, the first step is to mount the painting on thin card, using a solid gluestick in order to avoid crinkling the paper by wetting it. Scaled-down picture mouldings in plain or gilded wood can be chosen to suit the style of the picture.

You will need a mini mitre box and saw to cut the mouldings and mitre the corners. Instructions for using a mitre box and saw are given below. All the pictures in the classical art gallery (page 83) were cut out and framed using this method.

PROJECT

FRAMING PICTURES

1 Cut out your chosen picture and glue on to a piece of thin white card using solid gluestick, allowing a wide border all round.

2 Using a piece of the picture-frame moulding as a guide, lay it in place along each side of the picture in turn and draw along it with a pencil to mark out the finished dimensions of the frame on the card. Trim the card to this size.

3 Cut the mouldings using a mitre box and saw. The opposite sides of the frame must be precisely the same length for a good fit. After cutting the first piece, mark the length for the opposite side with a very sharp pencil before cutting. Repeat the process for the other two opposing sides.

4 Glue the mouldings around the picture on top of the spare card. Smear each piece of moulding with all-purpose glue and leave until slightly tacky before fixing: this will avoid the danger of getting any glue on the picture itself.

Note: The edges of the white card must be coloured or gilded to match the picture-frame moulding used. Use a gold pen or a coloured crayon.

BASIC TECHNIQUES

USING A MITRE BOX AND SAW

How to cut the mitred corners for a picture frame, window frame, door frame or fireplace.

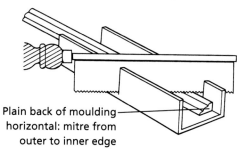

Plain back of moulding horizontal: mitre from outer to inner edge

How to cut corners for skirting, cornice and dado.

Plain back of moulding upright

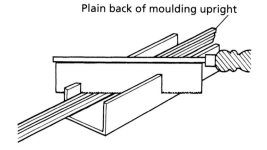

CLASSICAL SCULPTURE

The purpose of a formal gallery is to show off the collection: walls should be colour-washed to provide a background but not distract from the exhibits.

A gallery devoted to classical sculpture may be arranged in a room with Georgian-style decorations. Cornice and dado rail and a marble or tiled floor will be suitable, while the inclusion of marbled columns can add an extra dimension.

MARBLE COLUMNS

Wooden or plaster columns and capitals can be bought ready to paint as marble. If the back of the column cannot be seen, as in the sculpture gallery below, another method of simulating marble is to cover the column with thin marble-patterned card. Join at the centre back and glue it firmly in place.

ABOVE *Classical sculpture seen through a window of the gallery, which is set in a Georgian-style dolls' house. Ionic columns on either side of the pedimented doorway reinforce the striking effect of the sculpture on view.*

ABOVE *A formal sculpture gallery based on a museum example. Walls and floor are almost covered with plaster mouldings, marble statues (simulated in cast resin) and assorted pedestals, plinths and busts. If you fix the exhibits in place with Blu-tack it will be easy to rearrange them when you wish to provide a new perspective.*

Paint the capitals and bases so that they match one of the colours in the marbling.

Reeded columns are another idea: try using round dowelling and covering with fine corrugated card. Ensure that the join is at an indentation in the card, not a ridge, so that even if it can be seen it will not show up when painted. Paint reeded columns as stone, with light grey or stone matt-finish model enamel or with an acrylic paint mix.

Craftspeople make both classical and modern sculpture, cast most commonly in plaster or resin, but sometimes even in bronze. Look for quality in both the carving and in the material used. Busts and columns made of resin will be already coloured to resemble marble; plaster friezes and pediments can be painted using acrylic paints.

CHOOSING A BASE

Sculpture looks best if mounted on a pedestal or plinth: it is essential to choose the size and shape to suit the proportions of the piece.

AN EIGHTEENTH-CENTURY SCULPTURE ROOM

In the eighteenth century many gentlemen returned from the Grand Tour of Europe with sculpture and paintings, and these would be arranged in a room especially designated for the purpose of showing off their splendid souvenirs.

Such a room will be more domestic in feeling than the formal gallery devoted solely to painting or sculpture. Plain walls can be painted in Adam green or blue or in a stronger colour known as 'picture gallery red'. Modern paint ranges reproduce accurate versions of these historic colours, and they can be bought in small sample pots.

ABOVE *An instantly recognizable bust of William Shakespeare, reading from one of his plays. The bust is based on a likeness in the church in Stratford-upon-Avon where he was buried.*

ABOVE *Pedestals include two wedding cake pillars. These are inexpensive to buy, and they can be useful where height is required.*

ABOVE *This room might have been created by an aristocratic collector who would want an original and striking setting for his works of art. Note the use of skirtings made from thin black corrugated card: black marbled card would also be suitable. Sculpture and framed paintings might both be included in a home, rather than a formal gallery collection. A frieze can be simulated in card.*

ABOVE *Plaster mouldings and other materials used in the sculpture room shown above.*

ABOVE *A miniature of* The Little Dancer *by Degas, cast in bronze: it might be the focus of attention in an early twentieth-century sculpture gallery.*

ABOVE *This magnificent miniature of Donatello's David would take pride of place in any collection. It was cast in bronze, by the same lost wax method used to cast a full-size figure.*

LEFT *Mass-produced metal models can be transformed with paint. The Chinese horse has been painted to resemble jade, using pale green model enamel followed by a coat of varnish. The ochre-coloured plinth is made in cast resin.*

HOW TO MAKE A MARBLE FIREPLACE

This fireplace is designed to complement the sculpture rather than to house a grate, and it is easy to make.

1 Cut and join mouldings as shown on page 86.

2 For the marbled effect, first paint with cream or ivory model enamel.

3 To simulate veining, take a fine brush, dilute a little brown or grey model enamel with the creamy base colour, and feather on lightly, smudging a little here and there. It takes only a few minutes to produce a realistic effect. If you are uncertain about the painting, search out pictures of real marble, which naturally forms many patterns, and copy one you like.

4 Back the fireplace with black card. Cut the card long enough to be bent forward at the base to form a hearth, so that there is no possibility of a join showing.

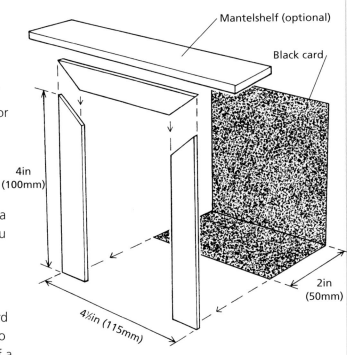

Mantelshelf (optional)

Black card

4in (100mm)

4½in (115mm)

2in (50mm)

LEFT *Symmetrical arrangements were admired in the late Georgian period. Paintings and plaster casts can be arranged in pairs.*

ORIENTAL SCULPTURE

An original setting may incorporate something a little unusual for a dolls' house hobbyist. Your choice will be governed by the particular piece that you wish to display separately from your main collection of miniatures. It could be an American Indian artefact, a Mexican carving, a Chinese jade figure or an exquisitely beautiful shell. Foreign travel, reference books and your imagination will all provide ideas which you can use.

My own example is oriental sculpture, which appeals to many westerners who have come to appreciate the serenity and stillness associated with Buddhist images. Miniature Buddhas and other carvings may be found in tourist and museum shops which feature Asiatic art: they range from basic metal casts to gilded statues of great beauty.

Inexpensive 'stone' figures from India can be left plain, as they look natural in small size. Very cheap metal and plastic figures can be easily, and effectively, transformed by gilding (see page 94).

Buddhist temples vary, depending on the school of Buddhism practised. They can be vast stone spaces, bare and awe-inspiring, with a gigantic Buddha figure at one end. In Tibet they are more often highly decorated, with a jewelled throne for the figure and with thangkas (traditional paintings on cloth) hung on the outside of the building. For the miniaturist an adaptation of this second option allows more scope, and can give rise to an imaginary scene which will reflect a spirit of calm.

Thangka paintings are colourful, lively and very exotic to western eyes. They show numerous images and can tell a complex story which may be difficult to fathom. Postcard size reproductions of thangkas can be found in shops catering for Tibetan people, as well as in museum shops.

It is possible to decorate a temple using inexpensive materials. It will need no furniture; texture and colour will provide sufficient interest. Paper the walls

ABOVE *Time for a change! This gallery devoted to oriental sculpture was used previously to show classical paintings. (See page 83) Plaster mouldings in a frieze below the cornice have been added to complement the sculpture.*

ABOVE *A Buddhist temple: the open top of the room box is covered with a bronze, self-patterned and semi-transparent flowerwrap paper which allows light to filter from above. Prayer flags made of paper are representational only, as they are normally hung on the outside of the building and would have inscriptions written on them. For simplicity, mine do not.*

ABOVE *Art paper and giftwrap form the basis for the decorative scheme of the temple. Gold-painted rocks add an exotic touch.*

with thick, creamy-gold woven papyrus from an art materials shop. The floor can be covered with patterned giftwrap in shades of orange and gold.

Prayer flags will suggest movement. Hang orange and yellow flags along each side wall. Suspend them from long green stalks cut from artificial flower sprays, to resemble bamboo poles. Cut the flags from ribbon or paper, roll one end of the flag around the 'pole' and secure with all-purpose glue such as UHU. Space the flags at intervals along the pole.

Hang the poles, complete with attached flags, on brackets hung over the side walls. A simple bracket support can be made from a short length of the flower stalk, bent to make a U-shape. Use metal brackets if preferred, and paint them green so that they match the poles.

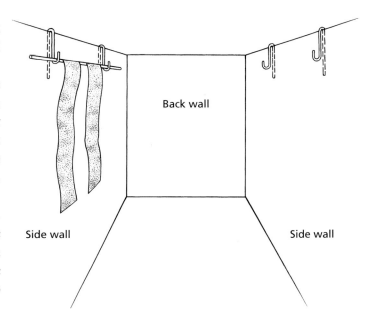

PROJECT

HOW TO GILD FIGURES

A gold or silver marker pen (of the kind that needs to be shaken before and during use) works well on metal, cast resin or plastic. It is worth practising how to use these pens before you begin.

1 Shake the pen vigorously. Then remove the cap and press the point down firmly on to some thick paper to start the metallic ink flowing.

2 Repeat this sequence at intervals during application.

3 Press down firmly to eject a blob of gold or silver which can be spread over the adjacent surface and into crevices with the point of the pen.

4 Take care when gilding faces: it is best to dip the pen into a blob ejected on to paper and then transfer a small amount to make fine lines.

5 The metallic ink dries reasonably quickly, but to avoid smudging play safe by leaving it for half an hour before touching.

Special furniture

At the very highest level of the maker's skill, unique furniture is not simply intended to be displayed in dolls' houses but may be destined for permanent exhibition in a museum. Alternatively, it may become part of a specialist collection belonging to someone who can afford and treasure such superlative work.

Few of us may own such pieces, but we can all admire them: it is inspiring to see just what can be achieved by the dedicated maker.

Cabinets and bureaux are commonly chosen for reproduction, because even in full scale they are among the most difficult and complicated pieces of furniture to make. They become increasingly so as the scale is reduced, allowing the miniaturist to test his skills to the utmost; to include marquetry or parquetry using rare and unusual woods and recycled ivory; to execute minute carving; or to paint detailed scenes that are revealed only when cabinet doors are opened.

Writing desks incorporating metalwork in the form of delicate rails and working locks may include secret drawers, concealed in inner compartments that open with a touch. Table tops may be tesselated in minute fragments of marble, or inlaid with mother-of-pearl or semi-precious stones. Musical instruments will be veneered in satinwood and boxwood, cross-banded with rosewood, ebony or tulipwood, and then finished with gold leaf.

The examples shown in the following pages represent some of the finest miniature furniture ever to be made in 1/12. They are all based on historically documented pieces, and for some the approximate date of the original is given.

RIGHT *A German bureau cabinet made by John Davenport in walnut with marquetry picture. The piece has a working lock on the desk flap.*

ABOVE *A Spanish chest on stand by John Davenport, made in rosewood with ivory fretwork.*

ABOVE *A Victorian table-desk by John Davenport, made in rosewood with floral designs in recycled ivory.*

ABOVE *An English cabinet on stand by Barry Hipwell: oyster veneered in laburnum, with legs in rosewood.*

ABOVE *An Antwerp cabinet on stand by Barry Hipwell, made in ebony with floral marquetry decoration. The original was circa 1700.*

RIGHT *An English fifteenth-century boarded chest with carved front by David Hurley.*

ABOVE *An Elizabethan/Jacobean court cupboard, elaborately carved in pearwood by David Hurley. In miniature scale the grain size resembles the original oak.*

ABOVE *An Italian folding chair of the late sixteenth or early seventeenth century. It is made by Ivan Turner in walnut and inlaid with ivory.*

LEFT *Elizabethan 'Seadog' table from Hardwick Hall in Derbyshire, England. The top is inlaid with semi-precious stones to represent the marble pieces in the original table. Maker: Ivan Turner.*

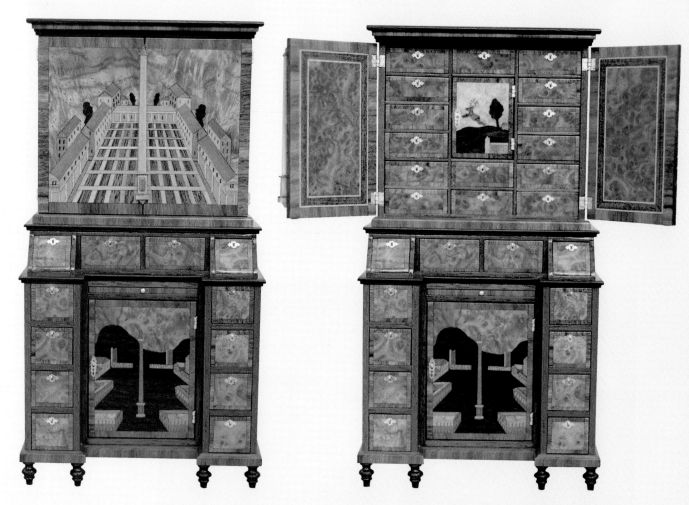

ABOVE *German cabinet/bureau with marquetry architectural scenes by Geoffrey Wonnacott, circa 1775.*

ABOVE *Inside, the same cabinet has a splendid array of working drawers.*

RIGHT *A nineteenth-century double action pedal harp by Alan McKirdy, finished in black lacquer and gold leaf in the 'Grecian' pattern.*

ABOVE *English cabinet on stand circa 1775, depicting scenes of British castles and abbeys. Made by Geoffrey Wonnacott.*

ABOVE Irish eighteenth-century breakfront bookcase with glazing in Gothick style, made by Michael Walton.

LEFT This late eighteenth-century demi-lune commode, made in mahogany and inlaid with amboyna, boxwood and ebony with rosewood crossbanding, is by Michael Walton.

ROOM BOXES FOR INDIVIDUAL SETTINGS

4

RIGHT *A space-saving idea: a shallow decorative picture box to hang on a wall, in late seventeenth-century William and Mary style. Typical of the period are the panelled wall, the reeded pilasters with gilded capitals and bases, the marble fireplace and the symmetrically arranged brackets to hold Delft blue-and-white pots.*

A room box can be an ideal starting point for a beginner, since it provides an opportunity to practise decorating and design skills before beginning to tackle a complete dolls' house. For the more advanced hobbyist it can be a good way to try out unusual ideas. It takes up little space and is sufficient for a shop or a small specialist collection.

A single room setting also make an excellent project for a group, such as a dolls' house club. With each member contributing a special skill, the completed scene may contain exemplary painting, needlework and woodwork which individuals might not be able to achieve on their own.

RIGHT *A joint project by a dolls' house club, this Adam library incorporates details from two famous rooms designed by Robert Adam at Mellerstain in Scotland and Kenwood in London. Great attention has been paid to reproducing authentic details.*

ABOVE *The outside of the Adam library is designed to complement the interior. It is painted to resemble the golden sandstone which Adam used for much of his building work. Windows and a pediment also enhance the effect.*

ABOVE *This large room box is 21in (530mm) wide, 12in (305mm) high and 15¼in (385mm) deep including the rear corridor. It is also available in kit form, with or without panelling, and lighting can be fitted to illuminate the background.*

Undecorated wooden room boxes are widely available, both ready-built and in kit form. Most have a hinged or lift-off perspex or glass front to keep the contents secure and dust-free. Some have a choice of period style doors and windows to be fitted at the back or sides, and they can also be wired for lighting.

ABOVE *The completed room ready for decoration, with panelling fitted and rear corridor lit.*

A typical room box will be the size of an average dolls' house room, measuring approximately 15in (380mm) wide, 10in (255mm) high and 11in (280mm) deep. Double boxes with two rooms side by side can also be purchased. Smaller boxes designed to hang on a wall will have less depth than freestanding versions.

You may prefer to buy a professionally-made wooden box to house a permanent arrangement, but if your woodworking skills are good enough the alternative is to design and make your own.

Another variation on the professionally-made room box is to construct a rear 'corridor' behind the main room so that an additional scene can be arranged. Windows and a door in an inner back wall will allow viewers a tantalising glimpse of the background scene.

FLOORING

Floor covering can be fixed to a card base before it is fitted into the room box, making it easy to change at a later stage if you wish. Start with paper or thin card, perhaps upgrading to tiles or a carpet at a later stage.

DECORATING A PANELLED ROOM

A Georgian panelled room can be treated in several different ways. Eighteenth-century panelling was always painted, but in the early Georgian period colours were limited. They have a tendency to make dolls' house-size rooms dark, as did the originals.

Setting the scene in the mid-Georgian era, on the other hand, gives an opportunity to use soft blue and white. Faux marble painted decoration added a fashionable look and this effect is simple to achieve in miniature, either with paint or simulated with marbled card. (For a marbled paint finish see page 91.)

It is essential to use masking tape to cover adjacent surfaces when adding a marbled paint finish to a frieze. Test out colours on card first to try variations on your faux marble before deciding on the pattern.

ABOVE *Different sizes of paint brush are needed to decorate the room. Smooth the wood before you begin painting, using glass finishing paper wrapped round a block of wood.*

LEFT *The inner back wall of the room shown on page 103 has been lifted out so that a backdrop can be arranged. Here an art gallery print has been used and fitted in position so that it will be seen to best advantage through the windows.*

LEFT *The panelled room is almost ready but the door still lacks a doorknob, which will be added later. The floorboards have been given a satin-finish varnish. The marbled frieze fills the space below the cornice.*

RIGHT *In a scene set behind the windows, the battle still rages, but Napoleon is defeated. Outside, an officer of the 95th Rifles foils a belated rescue attempt. This is not historically accurate, but fun for a miniaturist who is interested in the Napoleonic wars.*

BELOW *On the wall above the gilded console table, the painting shows the taking of a French 'eagle' at Waterloo. Like the painting of Wellington at the other end of the room, the picture was cut from a museum postcard and framed in gilt moulding.*

In the Georgian period, the cornice was often treated as part of the wall rather than painted the same as the ceiling, but this is a matter of personal preference. The window glazing bars and the fireplace can be painted off-white.

For my second version of an early nineteenth-century panelled room, the decorations are still elegant but they have become more formal. The walls have been repainted a mid blue-green from a range of historic paint shades. An ornate plaster ceiling and frieze have been provided, using an embossed dolls' house paper with a scaled-down plasterwork design. The fireplace is now painted to simulate French marble. A Napoleonic torchère and a marble-topped console table provide a touch of grandeur.

You can arrange any scene in order to reflect your own particular interests. Here the decorations and furniture have been changed in order to create a fictional background of the appropriate period for a genuine historic event: the scene is set for the Emperor Napoleon's abdication.

This setting also shows that military models and dolls' house rooms can work well together. Military model figures are not generally in 1/12, but provided the scale is reasonably close the effect will be good. Smaller figures, for instance, can be used to change the perspective and add a feeling of distance to a background scene.

PLAIN WALLS

For plain coloured interior walls, use artists' mounting board (Daler board, etc.) to make an inner lining to your room box shell. There is a huge range of colours, which includes silk finish and mottled effects.

Cut the board to fit inside the room box shell. Put the back wall in first, then the side walls, so that the join will be invisible. Attach with double-sided tape along the edges only, then it will be easy to change the decorations later if you wish.

PROJECT

HOW TO MAKE A SIMPLE ROOM BOX

If you plan to experiment with a number of different arrangements before deciding on finished style and decorations, it is economical to make a room box with an open front from ³⁄₁₆in (5mm) foamboard (available from stockists of art materials and good stationers).

Foamboard is strong and rigid and very light in weight, making it easy to carry around or take to club meetings. Most of the settings in this chapter were arranged in room boxes of varying sizes made in this material.

1 Decide on the size of the room.

2 Measure and cut the foamboard, making sure that the edges are straight and the corners square. Straight edges are easy to achieve if you use a self-healing cutting mat which will be marked with a grid of squares, and use a craft knife and raised-edge metal ruler.

3 Cut a floor, a back wall, two side walls and a ceiling (optional). Suggested measurements are given on the diagram but can be varied depending on your requirements.

4 Glue the pieces together, following the sequence shown in the diagram. An all-purpose adhesive such as UHU works well on foamboard: run a thin trail of glue along one edge only and press against the piece to be joined on. Hold together for a minute or two to bond firmly together. Wipe off any excess glue immediately.

5 To finish the box, you might like to paint the outside to complement the interior decorations. Use two coats of water-based emulsion paint or satin-finish decorator's paint.

Cutting note: the side walls are fixed to the floor and edges of the back wall and should be cut ³⁄₁₆in (5mm) longer than the floor to allow for this. The ceiling will be fitted on top of the back and side walls, so needs to be cut ⅜in (10mm) wider and ³⁄₁₆in (5mm) longer than the floor to allow for the thickness of the walls. The ceiling can be added after interior decorations are completed if preferred.

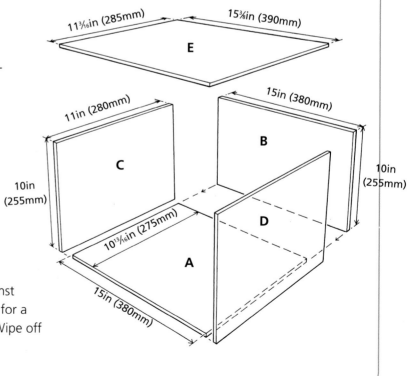

11³⁄₁₆in (285mm)   15⅜in (390mm)   E

11in (280mm)   C   15in (380mm)   B

10in (255mm)   10in (255mm)

10¹³⁄₁₆in (275mm)   D

A   15in (380mm)

TWO LITTLE SHOPS

Some specialized collections will look their best in a shop setting: hats and food are both particularly suitable, while furniture and ornaments can easily be incorporated into an antique shop, with the added bonus that the stock can be changed as items are moved either into a dolls' house or a designated room setting. My two examples – one Turkish, the other Japanese – are set in open-fronted room boxes.

A TURKISH CARPET EMPORIUM

A Turkish carpet emporium is a simple but effective way to show off miniature woven carpets. These are inexpensive and are available in dolls' house shops, museum shops and tourist outlets in a seemingly inexhaustible selection of designs and sizes. You will

ABOVE *Include as many carpets as you can. Carpets rolled in the corner are paper cutouts from magazines. They might be replaced by real miniature carpets as the collection grows.*

ABOVE *The shop is based on those in the Grand Bazaar in Istanbul, where there are rows of carpet sellers' stalls with their wares spilling out on to the ground in front. Cream woollen fringed braid provides a suitably ethnic hanging to finish off the stall.*

ABOVE *A 1/12 pewter coffee pot and two small glasses in silver filigree holders are set out on the table. The low stools are adapted from the lid and base of a small soapstone pot, topped with buttons in suitably oriental designs.*

see similar carpets used in rooms pictured throughout this book, as they fit in well with most periods and with most styles.

A plain background is best, as the carpets will make a colourful display. Use a white textured paper for the walls, or paint plain white if preferred.

One essential when haggling for a carpet in a bazaar is some refreshment, as the process is likely to take a long time. A low table can be made from a circle of card glued to a round base about 1½in (40mm) high. I used a picture of an Islamic plate to make the table top.

RIGHT *A portrait of a Turkish potentate on the shop wall makes an additional point of interest. This striking painting, cut from an exhibition listing, is framed handsomely in gilt.*

A JAPANESE SHOP

A colourful shop of the sort designed to attract tourists can be filled with holiday souvenirs for the visitor to buy. This busy shop layout will contrast with the sparse interior of any domestic Japanese room, where colour is generally kept to a minimum and anything not in use is stored neatly in cupboards and concealed behind sliding doors.

To make an authentic background for the objects on display, use a Japanese art paper: a selection of designs is usually available in art supplies shops or from stockists of art papers. The indigo blue patterned paper used on the walls is a good example.

Tatami matting is simulated by using corrugated card. In a Japanese home this would consist of mats placed together, each of them edged in black, but in

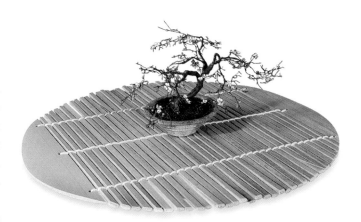

ABOVE *Realistic cherry blossom, made in metal, is displayed on a bamboo table mat.*

a miniature shop where so much of the floor will be covered by the stock it can be laid as a single sheet. Plain card will not give the right effect: use a water-based emulsion to paint it buff or light grey.

ABOVE *An open-fronted room box benefits from some trimming around the front edges to make a frame for the scene inside. This room is edged with a flimsy, semi-transparent Japanese white-on-white paper. The paper is creased into wings at the sides to suggest the folds of a kimono.*

ABOVE *In the Japanese shop try to provide a variety of levels to display goods: a low box or table can be used to draw attention to special merchandise.*

LEFT *Japanese prints appeal to art connoisseurs and tourists alike. Frame catalogue prints in thin black wood (see pages 84-86 for framing ideas and instructions). Alternatively, they can be mounted on black card, leaving a border showing to provide a mount.*

ABOVE *A mini-kimono which was attached to a greetings card (from the British Museum) is the perfect size to display in the shop.*

HINT

To give a worn effect to the matting, use black corrugated card and rub off some of the paint before it dries to give a patchy finish.

A RUSSIAN ROOM

The traditional Russian 'izba' is a wooden peasant cottage. Sadly, most of these have now disappeared to be replaced by tiny apartments in concrete blocks, although these, too, will be full of the colour and warmth which Russians consider important.

Whatever the size of the room, an essential feature is the stove. It is huge – and needs to be, in order to combat the sub-zero winter temperatures outside. In former times the stove in a peasant home was often a massive rectangular affair which filled a great part of the room, with a curtained shelf on top for sleeping. Today a cylindrical stove is more common.

To make the Russian stove, use an earthenware pastel burner. Mount it on a round box and, for extra height, top it with a second round box. Use the card centre from a kitchen paper roll as the chimney: it can be cut to fit the height of the room. Cover it with thin card to provide a smooth finish, and glue

ABOVE *The colourful lace-edged coverlet is a machine-embroidered fabric tablemat. Plain red fabric is used as a background for a variety of lace patterns.*

ABOVE *Wooden mouldings (purchased from a DIY store) simulate the carved wood which is always in evidence in Russian homes.*

on with the join at the back where it will not show. Glue the sections together and paint with white matt-finish paint.

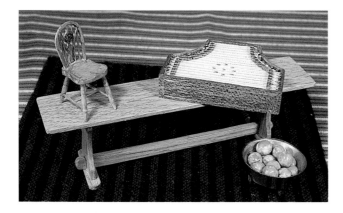

ABOVE *Woodcarving and music are popular Russian pastimes. Evidence of these activities can be arranged in a corner.*

ABOVE *The completed Russian stove in a corner of the room. A bench is placed nearby for warmth.*

An icon in a special corner was essential, with a candle placed nearby. Some Russians like to amass a collection, and for the miniaturist this is a good decorative idea.

Because of the intense cold outside, every inch of the floor would be covered by overlapping patterned rugs and small carpets. Richly coloured woollen or wool mixture dress fabrics are suitable to simulate the carpets.

The best (and possibly only) bed would be used in the daytime to show off a fine display of hand-worked and lace-trimmed textiles, in which red and white traditionally feature. Woven fabric or a small embroidered carpet should be hung over the bed, both as decoration and to give an extra feeling of warmth. Scraps of lace, ribbon and embroidered fabric will simulate the beautifully laundered textiles and hand embroidery which are displayed proudly in most Russian homes.

ABOVE *Icons glow against the dark green wall. The ones in this room are card cut-outs, but it is sometimes possible to find miniature wooden icons suitable for a 1/12 setting.*

HOLIDAY
INSPIRATIONS

5

RIGHT *The shuttered windows high up on the side walls of this Indian courtyard are painted in bright blue and green. You can make it look a little shabby by rubbing off small patches of paint before it dries.*

A holiday location can provide inspiration for an interesting miniature room or even a complete dolls' house. This will bring a remembered holiday to life more vividly than any photograph – or it may encourage you to visit that exotic location you have always planned to see for yourself.

The scenes I have chosen include courtyards as well as rooms, and they can be arranged in single or double settings. Holidays in different climates give us an insight into living arrangements in distant parts of the globe, and can provide many ideas for original miniaturized schemes which may be a new challenge but which will also be interesting to arrange.

Paint colours and textiles can play a big part in such settings. Colours and patterns used in hot climates are often much brighter than those in cool western countries: think of brilliant, gold-edged Indian sari fabrics, the delicate hand-embroidered silk hangings of China or the patterns and textures of Moroccan cushions.

A specialist dolls' house shop is the obvious place to find beautiful furniture for period or modern rooms. Arranging a more exotic room will give a different shopping experience as you search for ribbons and braids, greeting cards and small souvenirs from tourist and gift shops and even from department stores. You will be able to make simple furniture and decorate with these materials.

A SEASIDE COTTAGE

Most people remember their earliest seaside holiday, so my first choice is a cottage-style seaside home. Fishermen's cottages in both Britain and America are updated with the addition of modern plumbing to make desirable summer 'lets' for holiday-makers. The essence of any modernised cottage is simplicity. For a seaside home, concentrate on blue-and-white and keep bright colour accents to a minimum. Cover the walls with white rough-textured paper in order to give a plastered appearance: alternatively, paint with textured stencil paint. The floor can be covered with strong, thick paper in tones of blue. If you prefer carpet try plain blue felt or, alternatively, fit a planked floor for a natural look.

The nautical rug shown here is worked in needlepoint on fine canvas and was designed by an amateur maker. To design your own rug, draw a plan on graph paper and stitch it onto a size 18 or size 22 canvas, remembering that each square on the paper pattern represents a stitch over one thread on the canvas. The secret of success is to keep the design simple: stripes and a geometric pattern will make working straightforward.

To make a simulated needlework picture like the one hanging in the corner of the seaside room, draw a ship on Aida linen-weave fabric, using a very fine black pen. Frame the finished 'needlework' in plain picture frame moulding – either left uncoloured or varnished to darken it if you prefer.

Complete the room with a scattering of fishing nets, lobster pots and other fishy miniatures. Add buckets, spades and model ships to suggest that the eager holiday-makers have already arrived.

LEFT *A lobster pot and a rug with nautical design add interest to the seaside cottage.*

ABOVE *A room in a newly decorated holiday cottage, tidy and clean, ready for the holiday-makers to arrive. The traditional Orkney chair was professionally made. Scottish fishermen have made this type of chair for centuries, using driftwood collected from the beach, with the back and seat woven from seagrass or twine.*

ABOVE *Plain stripwood and blue-and-white striped cotton are used to make fitted sofas.*

HOW TO MAKE A SOFA

Fitted sofas upholstered in blue-and-white striped cotton are neat and give the appearance of having storage space beneath. Two sofas joined to form a corner unit make a striking feature.

1 Use a rigid box to form the sofa base, approximately 1in (25mm) high and perhaps 7-8in (170-210mm) long. Use the box for one sofa and the lid for the other, because the difference in length will be marginal.

2 Pad the tops with two thicknesses of foamboard, cut to fit the box and lid, and lightly glue together. Cover the foamboard by wrapping round with double thickness dressmaker's stiffening (Vilene) to give a soft but not squashy appearance. Turn the Vilene over the ends, neatening the corners by folding in a triangle at each corner as you do when packing a parcel, and glue in place underneath.

3 Cover with blue-and-white striped cotton, using the same method. Remember to match the stripes at the corner where the seats will join.

4 For the surround, use 1in (25mm) stripwood, cut to size and glued on to the box sides. Butt join at the corners – this is meant to look shipshape, not like expensive carpentry.

5 Finally, glue white piping cord all round the top edge of the wood strip. Cut the cord to the exact length to fit, twist the ends firmly together and fix with a dab of all-purpose glue to prevent the strands unravelling.

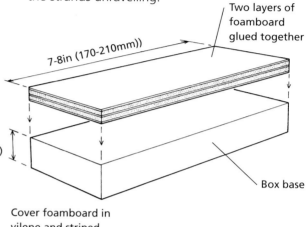

7-8in (170-210mm)

Two layers of foamboard glued together

1in (25mm)

Box base

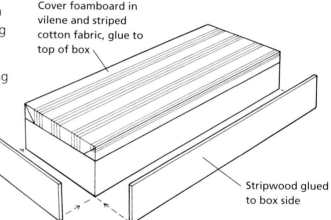

Cover foamboard in vilene and striped cotton fabric, glue to top of box

Stripwood glued to box side

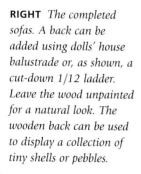

RIGHT *The completed sofas. A back can be added using dolls' house balustrade or, as shown, a cut-down 1/12 ladder. Leave the wood unpainted for a natural look. The wooden back can be used to display a collection of tiny shells or pebbles.*

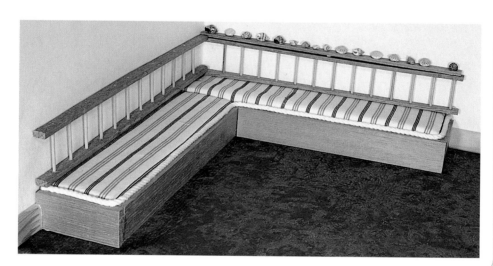

A MOROCCAN ROOM AND COURTYARD

Morocco has a special attraction for holiday-makers, and the local use of colour makes a strong impact. Wonderfully bright blues and greens, multi-coloured bead curtains, piles of red and orange spices in the market, pink walls and green plants combine in a glorious mix whose components never seem to clash. The miniaturist can enjoy reproducing some of the excitement and colour in a small space with only minimal expense.

A Moroccan room will appear more realistic if the paint doesn't look too new. To achieve the authentic slightly shabby effect, paint the door with a coat of mid-green model enamel and, when dry, follow with a coat of French blue. Don't apply the second colour too thoroughly, allowing some of the green to show through. Fix a strip of braid over the top of the door.

The floor can be tiled for coolness. You can either fit individual miniature ceramic tiles or, for economy, use a card simulation.

Almost all the furniture in a Moroccan room can be home-made or adapted from inexpensive objects. A low table, some low seating (large, squashy floor cushions, perhaps), a stove or storage unit, shelves and a battered cupboard are all you need.

ABOVE *In this Moroccan room, the floor is of shiny, dark green card with a faint pattern to give a tiled effect, and is partly covered by a small carpet. The walls are stippled pink. A vividly striped cotton fabric is draped over one wall and finished with a coarse-textured patterned braid.*

LEFT *Beads, buttons and scraps of braid and fabric will provide accessories for the Moroccan room.*

PROJECT

HOW TO MAKE A STORAGE UNIT

A white, free-standing storage unit is easy to make. The old-fashioned built-in stove is often converted into a storage unit, as nowadays small portable stoves are used for cooking. A good material to use is ⅛-³⁄₁₆in (3-5mm) foamboard, which will not need painting.

1 Measure and cut the foamboard pieces, following the diagram.

2 Cut 2 arched holes in the front of the lower part, and 1 larger arched hole in the front of the upper section. It will not matter if the holes are a little irregular in shape as this is an ethnic arrangement.

3 Glue the pieces together with all-purpose glue, being careful to centre the top section over the lower part.

1½in (45mm)

4½in (115mm)

4in (100mm)

2in (50mm)

1⅜in (35mm)

2in (50mm)

4¾in (120mm)

1⅞in (48mm)

4¾in (120mm)

1¾in (45mm)

Assembled unit

RIGHT *The completed storage unit. Buttons and jewellery bits and pieces simulate brass and copper dishes and pots.*

HINT

In this kind of project the exact size is not critical. It may also depend on the space you want to fill or the layout of the room. Adjust the measurements to suit your own requirements.

PROJECT

HOW TO MAKE A FLOOR CUSHION

1 Cut a strip of striped fabric about 5in (125mm) long by 2in (50mm) wide; turn in ¼in (6mm) on each long edge and then press or tack in place.

2 Fold twice to make a square, push in a small amount of dressmaker's wadding and slipstitch the edges together. Alternatively, use striped braid and there will be no need to turn in a side hem.

3 Pummel the cushions fairly fiercely to make them look squashy before putting them into the room.

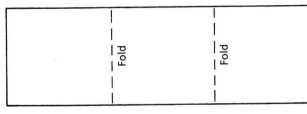

5in (125mm) approx.

2in (50mm)

¼in (6mm) turnings on all edges

Fold   Fold

Fold twice, insert stuffing, slipstitch sides and end

Dressmaker's wadding

Slipstitch edges together

To make a low table

Paint a small box and partially cover the sides with white braid or lace.

To make a low seat

Use a piece of balsa wood about 1in (25mm) high and 5in (125mm) or 6in (150mm) long as the base. Pad the top with dressmaker's wadding. Glue on a strip of braid to cover the top, and a narrower coarse braid around the sides.

HINT

Plastic can be painted successfully. A small perspex box can be painted in bright blue or green to make a wall unit.

LEFT *The Moroccan room, showing floor cushion and storage unit – and a battered-looking cupboard (see page 141)*

RIGHT *In the Moroccan courtyard the double doors are painted in a similar way to the inside room door, but the colours are varied slightly and a green-painted wooden lintel replaces the braid used inside. These doors were adapted from a cheap wardrobe. The main feature of the courtyard is the pool.*

A central courtyard surrounded by high walls is an oasis of cool shade in hot climates. The walls can be of rough-textured paper or card, or may be painted using textured stencil paint. The deep terracotta used on the side walls resembles reddish sandstone, while the sunset backdrop is a picture cut from a magazine, giving an extra dimension to the 'outdoor' courtyard. Although set in a room box, it is open-topped.

There are several alternatives for the floor: it can be tiled, painted as earth or covered with rough thick paper to look like white sand.

A pool can be any size you choose. It can be made from four pieces of stripwood, butt-joined and glued to a card or thin wood base. Paint both inside and outside as well as the top with bright turquoise acrylic paint. Fix on blue/green ceramic tiles, which are sold in craft shops, to make mosaics. You might use 'liquid water' paint for a realistic effect in the pool.

Tall palms in terracotta pots add to the oriental feeling of the courtyard and can be made very easily. A single spray of artificial greenery from a flower shop or a department store will be sufficient for several palms. Cut into suitable lengths and prune to shape. The main stem is generally wired: snip with wire cutters or pliers. The fronds can be trimmed with scissors. Alternatively, wide green plant ties can be cut and fringed to make thin palm leaves.

HINT

Complete picture frame kits measuring about 6 x 4in (150 x 100mm), consisting of a wooden base and ceramic or glass tiles to glue on, are widely available from craft shops and may be cheaper than buying the materials separately. An additional advantage of a kit is that it has the exact number of tiles to fit the frame provided.

ACCESSORIES

● Make a bead curtain to hang at the side of the door. Thread tiny multi-coloured glass beads on to nylon thread. Put the beads in a saucer, use a very fine needle, and it will be easy to pick them up one at a time with the tip of the needle.

● Make a large knot before threading on the first bead and, to make sure that it will not slip off, take the thread round and through twice before threading on the rest of the beads. Finish off using the same method with the last bead and, after knotting off, leave a long end of thread.

● Knot all the strands together to hang several rows of beads at the side of the door. To cover the whole door you will need many more rows: sew the ends on to narrow tape and either fix over the door with double-sided tape or glue in place. Cover the tape with a strip of braid.

● Make a hanging lamp from metal or glass beads intended for jewellery making. Thread on to a silk tasselled cord and suspend from thin chain hung across the top of the room.

● Provide a coffee pot. It can be of copper or brass: a design with a side handle is most suitable.

● Red lentils piled on a brass or copper dish will add a splash of additional colour. Use a button for the dish, and glue the lentils together in a pyramid shape to prevent them scattering around.

A MALTESE COURTYARD

One of the delights of visiting Malta is to look through tall wrought-iron gates and see that almost every house has its own internal courtyard with a few flowering plants and perhaps a statue or a fountain.

The flooring shown in the picture is a diagonal check green-and-white shiny paper. A hand-painted tile-effect floor is an alternative for which you can choose your own colour, and for such a small setting it will not be too time-consuming. Terracotta and cream, or turquoise and white, are often featured in Maltese courtyards.

Draw out squares or triangles on a sheet of card cut to fit the courtyard floor. Colour alternate squares or triangles using good quality art crayons. Fit masking tape to provide a clean edge between colours: the tape can be moved and refixed as you progress.

ABOVE *A Mediterranean-style patio pot is ideal for a Maltese courtyard.*

Walls on each side can be painted terracotta or stone colour, but the back wall might be painted pale blue to give a spacious look to the little scene. In Malta sculpture is likely to be religious in character, and the brackets on the walls in my courtyard feature angels.

The stained glass window used on the back wall is painted on silk and came from a handmade greetings card. Dolls' house-size stained glass designs to trace and colour yourself can be found in craft books.

The courtyard can be finished with plants, large garden pots and a 1/12 purchased fountain. A token 'well' is another possibility: the one shown is a soapstone box with a delicate lattice pattern. Such boxes are often made in India, and they can be found in gift or charity shops in suitable sizes.

LEFT *The Maltese courtyard is set in a very small room box, measuring only 7½in (190mm) deep, 9in (230mm) wide and 10½in (265mm) high, and is a reminder of a happy holiday.*

AN INDIAN ROOM AND COURTYARD

The diversity of decorative ideas used in Indian homes make it difficult to fix on one particular style for the hobbyist to reproduce, but it is very easy to create a miniature setting which will convey at least something of the colour and excitement of this warm and fascinating country.

There is no such thing as a typical Indian room: it can be as small or large as you wish. It might have mud floors and be decorated with traditional painted designs, or it could be a grand room based on a 'haveli' (mansion), a palace with marble floors or the epitome of ultra-modern luxury.

ABOVE *The ornate and colourful decorations make this room suitable for a maharajah. Orange tasselled braid and purple-and-gold cord finish the front of the room with a flourish. A courtyard can be arranged separately or combined in a double room box setting.*

LEFT *A choice of vividly coloured papers and ribbons for decoration.*

RIGHT *Colours and patterns from India. The white cut-outs are mounted on a bright orange card which makes a suitable contrast with the deep terracotta walls. White cotton lace-trimming is used as a border around the room.*

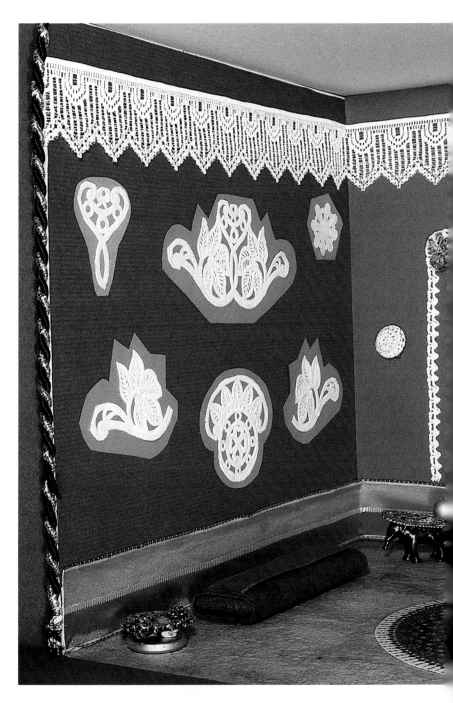

But whether it is small or large, plain or ornate, colour and decoration are what takes the Indian room into the realms of the extravagant. Colours positively sizzle: the juxtaposition of red, hot pink, bright green, orange and purple hues lifts the spirits.

Although both room and courtyard are decorated in a lavish style, it is not necessary to use expensive materials to achieve this effect. The floor and walls are covered with brightly coloured textured papers, while the (minimal) low furniture and the small wall decorations can be made with a combination of buttons, beads and fancy ribbons.

In Gujarat white plaster designs make a striking effect against terracotta walls. The designs are often lace-like, sometimes geometric, and can be used to emphasize archways and doors. This rustic style is now being used again by Indian architects to decorate ultra-modern buildings.

The decoration can be achieved in two ways. One is to draw your own designs with a white marker pen. Leaves and flowers, zig-zag borders and simplistic human figures are popular and not difficult to represent.

The more complex designs resemble the crystalline structure of a snowflake, and an easy way to simulate this is to cut out part of a white paper doyley.

LEFT *The roughly carved wooden tiger came from an oriental gift shop and has been painted to simulate a sandstone sculpture.*

HOW TO MAKE INDIAN STYLE ACCESSORIES

How to make low bench-like seats from corrugated packing card

1 Fold the card over several times to make a height of ½in (12mm) and a depth of about 1½in (40mm).

2 Trim to the desired length: the seats in the room shown are 4½in (115mm) long.

3 Fix the card with a dab of glue underneath.

To cover the seat base

1 Cover with non-fray velvet ribbon or a leather sample, with the suede side showing: leather and ribbon can both be cut neatly with sharp scissors.

2 Cut one large piece to the same length as the seat base and long enough to fold round it.

3 Join and glue underneath.

4 Finish the seat with a strip of moiré ribbon with Lurex edging.

How to make a canopy

1 Cut the card approximately 5in (130mm) high, and to fit the width of the room plus 10in (255mm).

2 Fold back 5in (130mm) at each end to glue to the sides of the box. A card top can be fixed on top.

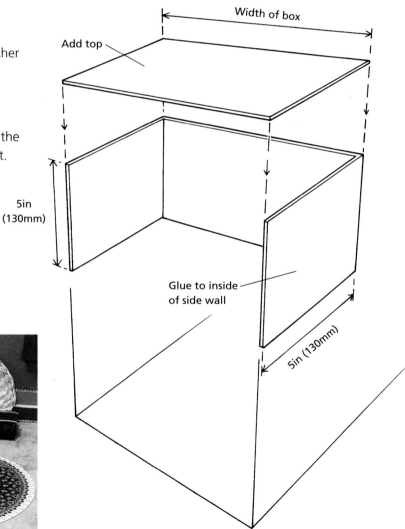

Width of box

Add top

5in (130mm)

Glue to inside of side wall

5in (130mm)

4 Rough up the surface slightly with a coarse glasspaper to make it resemble rough sandstone.

5 Cut a piece of shiny dark blue paper to fit inside the pool to simulate water.

6 Scatter with pink artificial flower petals or with small blossoms.

How to make the courtyard seating

Low seats are made in a similar way to the more formal ones in the main room but are covered with gold-trimmed Indian sari fabric.

1 Cut a piece of fabric twice the width of the seat base and long enough to wind around it several times.

2 Place the base in the centre of the fabric and fold over and over to pad and cover the base.

3 Fold the ends in neatly, making sure that some of the gold Lurex trim shows on top.

4 Glue the fabric ends underneath.

How to make the pool

Make a pool in a similar way to the one used in the Moroccan courtyard, but omit the tiles.

1 Cut four pieces of stripwood to make a rectangle approximately 6 in (150mm) x 4in (100mm).

2 Butt join and glue to a wooden or card base.

3 Paint with a mix of buff and pink water-based emulsion paint or an acrylic mix.

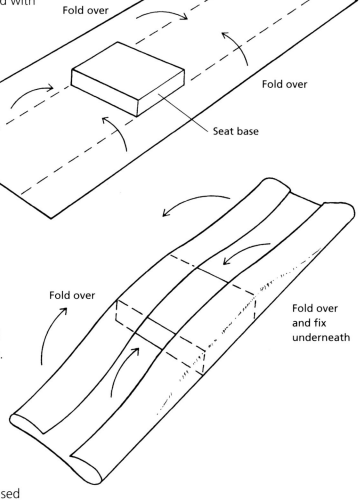

Fold over

Fold over

Seat base

Fold over

Fold over and fix underneath

Mount the white patterns on a roughly-cut card shape in a different shade from the colour of the main wall, and glue it in place so that you fashion a random design.

Steps are a feature of Indian courtyards. An arrangement of shallow steps can be graduated in size to form a raised platform for the seats on top of a series of steps. Make the steps from pieces of foam-board, covered with the same paper as the main floor or painted to match. For shade, fit a card canopy covered with the same paper as the back wall over the raised platform and seats.

ABOVE *The courtyard walls are lined with a pale pink paper with a corn-coloured rough fleck. The floor is covered with terracotta paper with an indistinct pattern resembling bricks. Alternatively, paint the floor with a light grey-brown mix to resemble hard-baked mud.*

LEFT *Materials used in the courtyard. The lid of an Indian wooden box with a typical openwork grille pattern is used as a door at the rear of the courtyard.*

6

Outdoor Scenes

RIGHT *The open door of a Tudor house shows a glimpse of a formal flower arrangement inside. Climbing roses are set in a small raised base at the side of the door to link the hall and the garden.*

A dolls' house may have a porch which can be used to link the interior with an outside space. A verandah or terrace can be treated as an extra room for garden furniture and potted plants. Even a small and drab base surrounding the house can be enlivened by the introduction of plants or garden tools.

Climbing plants can be attached to trellis on the house wall near a door or window, or fixed to a metal or wooden obelisk. Fix the support into a piece of florist's oasis to make a raised, grassy bed and dot with small flowers. This is easy to move around when you want to change the garden scene.

Medieval houses were sometimes fashioned from former monasteries. In a shady cloister flowering plants may be out of place, but the space can be used for livestock. Realistic miniature beasts and birds will appeal to the animal lover, and this provides a good opportunity to use them.

For a logpile, gather twigs of a suitable thickness from the garden and cut to the required length with a sharp knife. Glue the resulting logs together in a neat pile on a small wooden base. One coat of matt varnish will preserve the logs and prevent flaking.

Free-standing garden buildings can be placed on a terrace or paved area outside a dolls' house. They extend the selection of miniatures which can be included, while taking up little extra space.

ABOVE *An ancient half-timbered house with an exterior covered stairway also has room for a well, a dovecote, a water butt and a small barrel containing water lilies. Well-heads can be bought ready-made or to assemble from kits.*

ABOVE *The remnant of a cloister now has a new use as a chicken run, with other farm animals among the logpiles and bales of hay.*

ABOVE *This small wooden shed stands on a firm paved base which can be used for gardening tools and plants. The horseshoe over the door is a traditional touch, fixed to 'hold' luck.*

THE BRITISH GARDEN SHED

In Britain, gardening is a national pastime, and a potting shed is essential to raise seeds and shelter growing cuttings. A heated conservatory may be too expensive for most families (although, in miniature, a conservatory might replace the shed), but a small 'retreat' provides shelter and a place to work in bad weather. Its base will define the space to be used for plants or gardening equipment: cut a piece of plywood or medium density fibreboard (MDF) to the size you need, allowing at least 3in (75mm) all round the building.

● Provide paving by marking out squares and rectangles to resemble flagstones: paint with matt stone model enamel, or glue on sheet paving with a plasticised finish.

● For a lawn surround, railway modeller's grass with a peel-off backing is easy to cut and fit.

● For additional realism you may prefer to use ceramic or resin flagstones. To do this, measure the base wood carefully before cutting to make sure that the flagstones will fit exactly without trimming: it will look neater if entire flagstones are used.

The miniatures you put in your shed are a matter of personal choice – it has many other possible uses besides its primary role as a potting shed. Depending upon your current collection of miniatures, together

ABOVE *The traditional garden shed is made of timber with the door at one end. Most miniature sheds have a lift-off roof to allow access for the hobbyist to arrange the contents. The view into this shed through the open door shows an array of plants plus a variety of equipment for the gardener.*

with your plans for future purchases or things to make, it can be used to store garden furniture, tricycles and other children's toys, a pram or a pushchair. It might even provide a useful repository for spare furniture, especially broken items which may feature as junk 'awaiting removal' until you have sufficient spare time to repair them.

LEFT *A workbench equipped with a full set of tools will transform a potting shed into a tool shed for the keen woodworker. For the miniaturist there could be a bonus to this idea: the many small drawers give ample space to store tiny screws, hinges, sets of handles, glasspaper and mini drill bits, all of which may come in useful when working on a dolls' house project.*

ABOVE *Windows at the side of the shed allow a view through to the outside and provide light inside when the roof is in place. Hats and indoor games are stored in a corner near the door, ready for use.*

The shed can become a home office or workshop, using scaled-down office furniture and equipment, or you might like to fit it out as a toolshed, complete with workbench and miniature tools as well as the work in progress.

IDEAS FOR THE POTTING SHED

Although many of the objects in and around the shed may be purchased ready-made, there is plenty of scope for small things to make. If you are not a gardener yourself, take a look inside some of your neighbours' sheds and you will be amazed by how much they contain. Here are some ideas:

● To provide earth or compost for plantpots, 3/4-fill the pot with screwed-up paper, spread the top of the paper with glue and cover with fine tea from a teabag.

● Some plants look more attractive if they are surrounded by small pebbles. Glue a little paper around the base of the plant, spread with more glue and cover with sesame seeds.

● Make wooden boxes for bedding plants from balsa wood. Cut with scissors: all you need is a rectangle for the base and four strips of balsa glued on to form the sides.

● Puy lentils can be used to make gravel for box containers. Spread the base with glue and press the lentils firmly in place. The greenish-black colour is very attractive.

BELOW *Provided that it is carefully chosen, a piece of sculpture can add a touch of magic to even a small terrace or patio (see Garden Follies on opposite page). This classical bronze figure is copied from the marble* Nymph and Scorpion *by Bartolini, and on its own would furnish a small space.*

RIGHT *Oriental garden buildings held a particular attraction for English landowners in the eighteenth century, and there are still quite a few dotted around landscaped grounds today. This miniature version of the genre, with its trellised fencing and thatched roof, might be equally fascinating to the hobbyist who owns a large dolls' house and has space for a folly.*

GARDEN FOLLIES

For the miniaturist, siting statues and garden follies can be an enjoyable change after decorating a whole dolls' house. For the beginner, completing a setting for a gazebo or pavilion can be a rewarding entrée to the hobby before beginning on a larger project.

In the Georgian period a rotunda was often placed at the end of a long ride or on a grassy mound in the park of a stately home as a focal point. For the dolls' house owner it can become the focus of attention nearer to the house.

A garden terrace which can be attached to the wall of a dolls' house or stand on its own is another opportunity to extend display space and try out arrangements from different countries.

LEFT *Garden buildings of this kind developed from Italian architectural styles. This pleasant example is made of wood which has been painted and textured to look like weathered stone. An urn on a pedestal completes the picture.*

The terrace can be any size you choose, depending on what you want to use it for. In addition to a variety of plants and flowers, it can provide a place for outdoor eating or a play space for children which will allow you to provide toys or put a perambulator in a corner for a sleeping baby.

A FRENCH TERRACE FROM PROVENCE

Tall walls surrounding a French Provençal terrace will be made more interesting with the addition of shuttered windows and a doorway. Windows complete with shutters which open suit the Provençal style and can be purchased ready to fit.

ABOVE *A seat in a shady corner near the doorway is a resting place for doves. A tub of marguerites on either side and an orange tree in a Versailles planter reinforce the idea of a lazy afternoon in France.*

Alternatively, provide windows with closed shutters, made from white card and blue corrugated card (from craft shops). To simulate the effect of paint which has been bleached by strong sunlight, soften the colours with a wash of acrylic paint mix.

The doorway represents the entrance to an adjoining house. You can buy a door but, for economy, another possibility is to use a pair from a cheap wardrobe and paint them in French blue model enamel.

To make the doorway more imposing, steps to raise it can be cut from foamboard or balsa wood and then painted with matt stone model enamel. A surround of terracotta card or painted wood will enhance this impression.

FINISHING TOUCHES

● One or two sprays of artificial greenery can be used effectively as trailing plants against the walls.

● Choose regional plants, such as a hydrangea and an orange or lemon tree, to show off in containers.

● Add chairs and a table, a bottle of wine and glasses, and perhaps a long French loaf and cheese.

● Paint an inexpensive rush-seated chair, and add a garden hat and a basket of flowers to suggest that the terrace is used.

ABOVE *This typical Provençal terrace is set in a two-sided room box 17in (430mm) long and 15in (380mm) deep, made from foamboard. The walls are painted deep pink to represent adjacent house walls, and the base is covered with a thick, textured handmade paper in a sandy-grey colour. An alternative would be to pave the floor with the attractive hexagonal ceramic tiles which are common in France.*

ABOVE *Basic materials for the French terrace are inexpensive and easy to find.*

A GREEK ISLAND TERRACE

In Greece the striking combination of white houses and terraces set against the brilliant blue of sea and sky makes an overwhelming impression. Terraces straggle down thyme-clad hills in a random manner, partly because their walls make use of rocky outcrops as foundations.

To create such a setting from material which will cost nothing, use expanded polystyrene packing of the kind used to protect household appliances in transit. The moulded polystyrene is formed into ridges and curved shapes to fit round whatever was inside it originally, and this will provide a ready-made base for a hillside terrace.

Any gaps in the design can be filled in with thick card, providing a flat paved area which – painted with textured stencil paint – will provide a plausible representation of low ground-cover plants, either in a symmetrical planting of squares or, alternatively, as a dense covering. You could perhaps add plants in pots or a classical pediment or column.

Set the polystyrene base into a two-sided room box. Line the walls with bright blue-green picture mounting board which can be glued in place or fixed with double-sided Scotch tape. A three-sided room box can have one side wall painted with textured white paint to simulate an adjacent house wall.

You will need to make sure that the base of the polystyrene is level. Use wooden or rigid blocks as supports at strategic points to keep it steady. Arrange the supports so that the terrace simulates a sloping site, and fix them to the base of the room box with Blu-tack to keep everything securely in place.

When the base is firmly set up, cover any gaps round the sides with thick white card or foamboard to make a neat edge to the 'outdoor room'.

IDEAS TO COMPLETE THE GREEK TERRACE

● Keep to the blue-and-white theme in order to achieve maximum effect.

● Cut a small expanded polystyrene box in half to make a sofa (or a matching pair) as shown on page 68. For a sofa that is to be used uncovered outdoors, a slightly rough appearance is unimportant. Cover the seat with a long cushion of blue-and-white striped cotton.

● Add some greenery. Spiky Mediterranean plants may be cut from artificial flower leaves, trimmed to a suitable shape. Sprays of tiny blue flowers can be used as thyme or sea-lavender. Plant them in patio pots or make an extra box from polystyrene to fit against a wall, and fill it with blue flowers on short stalks.

LEFT *The part of the Greek terrace overlooking the sea is reserved as a refreshment area.*

● Chairs can be painted bright blue, while a plain white table will look more attractive if it is given a simulated mosaic top. One approach is to search through magazines for something of a suitable design and size, and glue it in place on the table top.

● Wine and glasses are essential in such a setting. Miniature glasses can be purchased ready-filled with 'wine' (made of coloured resin). To simulate the inevitable ouzo, part-fill plain glasses with cold weak tea set with gelatine.

ABOVE *The coarse-grained appearance of sparkling white expanded polystyrene used as a base makes a good 1/12 simulation of rough-hewn whitewashed stone.*

ABOVE *Simple materials combine to make a Greek terrace which will bear a remarkable resemblance to the real thing. A wedding cake pillar can represent an ancient stone column: a broken one can be used as an antique fragment.*

AN ENGLISH GARDEN TERRACE

Finally, here is an English garden terrace assembled from a kit. It is sufficiently easy for a beginner who has never tackled a kit before, as the trellis panels are supplied ready made up.

For simplicity, paint the base and baluster section with a coat of matt stone model enamel. The wooden structure should be stained and varnished before you glue the pieces together, to avoid the possibility of any glue spots on the untreated wood: these would show up as bare patches after staining. Wood dye can be applied with a dry cloth, but use a cotton bud or fine paintbrush to work the stain into the corners of the trellis.

Alternatively, spray-paint the wooden structure after assembly using a spray-paint designed for use on models. (See page 139.)

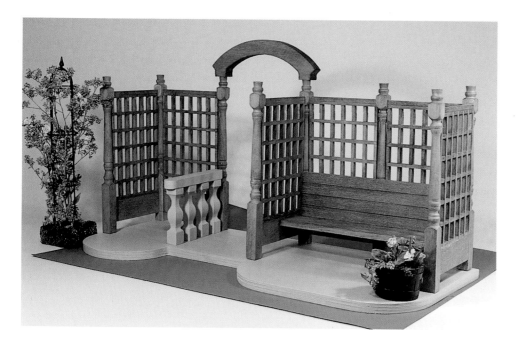

LEFT *A garden terrace made from a kit, ready for the addition of flowers and accessories. The wooden structure has been stained with medium oak wood dye, followed by a coat of matt varnish, to simulate the creosote traditionally used to weatherproof English fencing.*

LEFT *The garden setting can be changed to suit the seasons. An idyllic summery setting can include outdoor games and perhaps a picnic. For an autumnal scene, the ivy can be left on the trellis and the tubs changed to hold autumn plants. Later, a scattering of 'snow', a snowman and a sledge would transform it for winter.*

FURNITURE KITS AND PAINT TRANSFORMATIONS

ABOVE *Exuberant painting by a talented professional miniaturist turns an elaborately coffered ceiling into a work of art. This could inspire many hobbyists to take up painting, although perhaps on a more modest scale. A good way to begin is by painting furniture.*

Furniture of all kinds is shown and discussed in this book, to give a general picture of what is available for the hobbyist, from one-off masterpieces made to commission, through elaborate furniture of many styles and periods to simple pieces that can be made from humble materials by someone with no woodwork experience at all. There are options to suit all interests and all pockets.

This section suggests two economical methods of providing furniture and at the same time enjoying the pleasure of putting something together yourself. The first describes how to assemble furniture from kits, and the second how to transform inexpensive furniture with a variety of paint finishes.

Furniture kits

As a halfway stage towards actually making furniture, assembling a kit can be rewarding and will give you an idea of how furniture is put together. Choose your kit carefully: whether designed by a maker who has diversified or provided by a manufacturer who mass-produces a range of kits, it should be of good-quality wood or MDF and have clear assembly instructions.

Not all kit packs feature a picture of the finished piece, although this can be helpful to check that the

proportions are correct for the style. If not, see-through packs will enable you to check whether the wood is suitable for the design. The number of pieces to assemble should be a further guide to the ability level required.

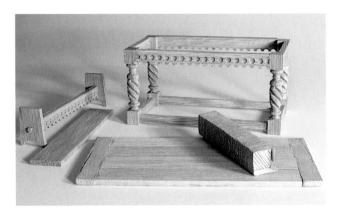

ABOVE *A kit set of Tudor table and benches, shown here part-assembled. The pieces are of good quality oak.*

ABOVE *The completed table and benches, shown here with a matching high-backed chair, look authentic: they have been stained with a medium oak wood stain and then polished.*

ABOVE *This simple kit is suitable for a beginner. The pieces are laser-cut and fit so well that glue is almost unnecessary. This version of a Lutyens garden seat is of MDF (medium density fibreboard) and can be spray-painted, but it is also available in cherry or spruce which can be polished or varnished.*

ABOVE *An example of an early nineteenth-century Biedermeier sofa from a large range of European furniture mass-produced by an American manufacturer specialising in kits. The piece is a good copy of the original well-proportioned sofa. Other examples made from kits are shown in the Biedermeier section on page 47.*

ABOVE *Victorian-style kitchen furniture which could be used equally well in a modern kitchen, depending on the finish chosen. The shelf unit has been given a distressed look by using an acrylic paint, and the chairs have been painted with a cheerful yellow which Vincent Van Gogh might have enjoyed. For a Victorian kitchen, the furniture could be stained and then polished or varnished.*

PAINT TRANSFORMATIONS

Adapting and transforming cheap furniture with a new paint finish is fun to do and costs little. A variety of such furniture is shown in rooms throughout this book. Occasionally the same piece is shown in both a conventional and a more unusual room, to demonstrate different uses. See if you can spot this dual-purpose furniture in the pictures.

Imported furniture, mainly made in Asia, is widely available and generally cheap. The shapes and styles are often good, if sometimes lacking in delicacy. The finish, on the other hand, is usually unsatisfactory, generally because unsuitable high-gloss varnish has been used and applied too thickly. Don't let this deter you: the piece can easily be transformed into something far more attractive.

When using spray paint, cover the surrounding area and work surface with layers of newspaper, make sure there is good ventilation, and place the object to be sprayed inside a large cardboard box. Spray paint which has been designed to use on small surfaces can be obtained from a model supplier. Car spray paint is much too thick for this purpose, and it would clog delicate wire mesh and any other small apertures. With each piece, the first step is to strip and clean all the surfaces.

ABOVE *Starting work: the cupboard as bought is stained with dark-coloured gloss varnish.*

STRIPPING AND CLEANING

1 Cover your work table with layers of newspaper. When using paint-stripper, keep a window open for good ventilation and always wear rubber gloves. A piece of rag should be kept handy for any mopping up that may be necessary.

2 Apply a proprietary paint-stripper and follow the instructions on the can, using wire wool and an old toothbrush to work the fluid into any carving or small corners.

3 When the varnish is removed, wipe the piece over with white spirit and leave it near an open window until the fumes evaporate.

● **OPTIONAL** The wood used in such miniatures is often a dark colour. If you are after a pale, distressed finish, apply slightly diluted household bleach. Wipe on plenty with a rag (again wearing rubber gloves to protect your hands) and leave for about 10 minutes. Wipe off the residue and leave the piece to dry in fresh air. Finally wipe over with a vinegar-and-water solution mixed about half-and-half, and leave it to dry thoroughly.

4 Smooth over gently with fine glasspaper, working in the direction of the grain, and wipe with a clean, smooth cloth to remove any dust. The piece is now ready to paint or stain.

FURNITURE TRANSFORMATIONS

Here are four examples of furniture transformations, with 'before' and 'after' pictures to reveal the effects which can be achieved when you wish to improve inexpensive furniture.

A LONGCASE CLOCK

1 Strip off and prepare the wood as detailed earlier.

2 Paint with one coat of matt green model enamel.

3 Leave until barely dry to the touch and then follow with a coat of bright green gloss enamel.

4 Wipe off patches of this second coat immediately with a cloth dipped in white spirit. This will tone down the green colours and leave some of the original wood colour showing through.

5 The paper clock face will not survive the use of paint stripper. The original modern clock face can be replaced by one in a more suitable style: pictured clock faces can be found in gift catalogues and advertisements in magazines. Glue on a new face and fit a small brass curtain ring as a surround.

A TALL CUPBOARD WITH OPEN SHELVES

1 Remove the plastic film from the door panels.

2 Strip off the varnish and smooth the wood both inside and out.

3 Paint the outside of the cupboard in your own colour choice.

4 Line the door panels with mesh. Miniature wire mesh can be bought. An alternative (as shown) is to use the slightly stretchy plastic mesh which is found around some wine bottles. Plastic mesh

ABOVE LEFT *Before: Apart from its poor finish, this is a nicely detailed longcase clock. The cresting on the top is a good feature and it even has a hanging brass pendulum inside, but the paper dial reproduces a modern clockface.* **RIGHT** *After: This clock can now be used as an antique (see page 52). A slightly distressed finish has been chosen.*

ABOVE LEFT *Before: This adaptable cupboard can be used as a china cabinet or to store linen so that the contents will be on show.* **RIGHT** *After: The cupboard has been repainted in French blue model enamel to use in a kitchen. If it is to be used on a landing or in a bedroom, you might want a more discreet colour, perhaps pale green or cream. The plastic film over the doors has been replaced with mesh.*

bags containing chocolates, fruit or cheeses are also suitable for the purpose.

5 Make a paper pattern to fit the inside of the door and cut the mesh exactly to size.

6 Apply a minute trail of all-purpose glue to the inner edges of the door panels with a wooden cocktail stick. Leave until tacky and then press the mesh firmly into place.

7 If the cupboard is to be used for food, paint the inside pale blue, a colour which has always been thought to deter flies. To display crockery, the shelves can be lined with wallpaper in the traditional way.

A HARP

1 Strip and prepare the piece as before, taking care to avoid damage to the stringing. Paint stripper will not damage brass fittings.

2 Repaint with satin-finish black model enamel: use a size 00 brush on the inner edges to avoid smudging paint on to the strings.

3 Add gold decoration with a gold marker pen. Shake the pen vigorously before and during use (as for the Buddhist sculpture on page 94).

A pattern of random swirls is easy to achieve and will look impressive. The top and base of the harp can be covered with gold.

AN OLD-FASHIONED CUPBOARD

This cupboard is shown in its original state, covered with brown varnish, on page 139.

1 Strip and prepare the piece as before.

2 To create a washed-out appearance, first undercoat with white water-based emulsion paint. Before it dries, wipe it off here and there with a rag to allow some bare wood to show through. Note that the areas with most obvious wear would be around the handles and the corners.

3 Apply a coat of mid-blue emulsion paint, painting lightly and again rubbing off here and there to allow both undercoat and bare wood to show through.

4 Finish with a coat of matt varnish to seal the paint.

HINT

The method of distressing used on the cupboard can be followed to produce a similar finish on new whitewood furniture for a modern setting. For this use leave minimal areas of bare wood showing. Cream over pale grey, or yellow over cream, are both popular with modern kitchen designers.

ABOVE LEFT *Before: The harp is nicely strung and even has brass foot pedals, but it is varnished in an unpleasant red-brown meant to represent mahogany.* **RIGHT** *After: The harp has been repainted black with gold decoration.*

ABOVE *This cupboard is intended to look old and battered, and has been given a pale-coloured distressed paint finish.*

ECONOMY HINTS

● Another way to make good use of cheap furniture is to take it apart and use sections to make doors and windows. The shuttered windows on the walls of the Indian courtyard on page 126 are made from part of a cupboard, and wardrobe doors have been re-used in both the Moroccan and French courtyards.

● When doors have been removed, a cupboard with shelves can be used as an open bookcase, or adapted to make an alcove to display ornaments. In this way, one piece of furniture will have two uses.

● White wire furniture made in China looks well in conservatories, in garden rooms or on terraces. It doesn't have to remain white, however, and you can transform the various pieces with spray paint to suit your particular setting.

These ideas for transforming inexpensive miniatures will, I hope, not only help you to enjoy yourself while achieving your planned result (saving money at the same time), but will inspire you to think of all sorts of ways to reinvent pieces for yourself.

This, after all, is only the start.

PROJECT

TRANSFORM METAL MINIATURES

Metallic paint can be used to make a plain pewter figure look like bronze.

1 Paint with one coat of dark brown model enamel.

2 Apply a top coat of bronze metallic model enamel, rubbing off here and there with a rag before it dries to reveal small patches of the duller brown.

3 When dry, buff up with a dry soft cloth.

ABOVE *The head of a girl shown in the French hall on page 52 was also painted using this method, but with a first coat of greenish-brown rather than dark brown.*

RIGHT *A pewter bust of Napoleon looks impressive when repainted as bronze and displayed on a mineral sample pedestal.*

LEFT *This imposing 'bronze' bust is displayed on a plain classical plinth.*

BASIC TOOLS AND MATERIALS

TOOLS

You will need the following basic tools to fit out rooms:

- Small screwdrivers in a selection of sizes.

- Bradawl (a pointed tool for starting a hole in wood to insert screws).

- Craft knife with replaceable blades.

- Transparent plastic ruler (useful for checking detail when marking out patterns).

- Metal ruler with a raised edge for use as a cutting guide.

- Self-healing cutting mat marked out with a squared grid.

- Metal mitre box and saw (eg X-Acto mitre box no. 7533 and knife handle no. 5 fitted with saw blade no. 239). Other makes are available, all of them of a fairly standard size, from suppliers of miniature tools.

- Small saw approximately 7in (180mm) long.

- Pencils (well-sharpened).

- Bulldog clips for holding parts together while glue sets.

- Masking tape.

- Magnifier for checking fine detail.

ABOVE *Tools and glues can be stored away neatly inside the dolls' house while work is in progress. An egg cup makes a useful container for tiny screws.*

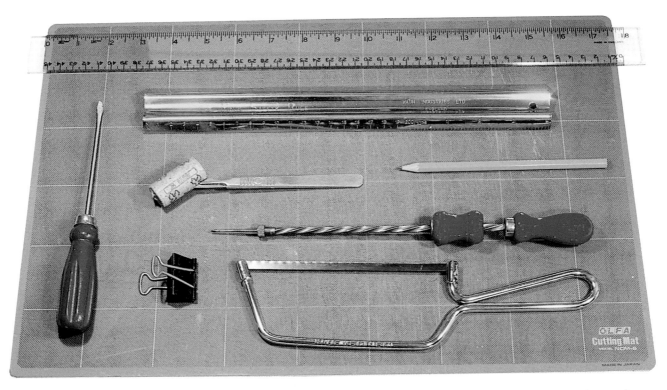

ABOVE *These tools are essential if you plan to add fixtures and fittings. From the top:* plastic and raised edge metal rulers, craft knife, pencil, small screwdriver, bradawl, bulldog clip, small saw.

SHARP TOOLS

Blades on craft knives must be changed frequently. They are inexpensive, and they work effectively only when they are sharp.

A good pair of scissors will be adequate for some purposes, but it is far more difficult to cut perfectly straight lines on paper or card. Using the grid on a cutting mat will save a great deal of time and trouble when cutting parallel edges on wallpaper, etc.

Sharpen pencils often, because the width of the line made by a blunt pencil will make measurements inaccurate.

SAFETY FIRST

Treat all cutting tools with respect

Rule 1 To avoid accidents, always check before you cut that your free hand is behind the blade and not in front of it.

Rule 2 Never use cutting tools if you are tired, when it becomes too easy to make a mistake. There is always another day.

Rule 3 Always put a craft knife down while you check or adjust the position of the work. It is easy to forget that you are holding it and to nick yourself.

ADHESIVES

Modern adhesives are not interchangeable and work best on the materials for which they are intended. This check list is a brief guide to what is suitable for different materials.

All-purpose clear adhesive For card, paper, wood, ceramics (eg UHU and Bostik).

PVA whitewood adhesive For permanent fixing of wood: once set, the bond cannot be undone. Evo-Stik Resin 'W' is widely available.

Rubber-based adhesive To attach ceramic tiles to card or wood. Do not use on fabric as this type of glue (eg Copydex) yellows with age.

Superglue To attach ceiling roses, etc. Also use for fixing metal to wood (metal feet, for example, attached to wooden legs on furniture) and to fix together very small parts.

Solid gluestick Generally preferable to paper glue, because it will not crinkle paper by over-wetting.

GLUE FUMES

Most glues produce fumes to some extent and it is essential to work in a well-ventilated room, preferably with the window open.

SUITABLE PAINTS FOR INTERIOR USE

Water-based emulsion paint Interior walls and ceilings and as an undercoat on thinner wooden mouldings.

Gloss paint Do not use.

Semi-matt paint (Satin finish or eggshell finish) Doors, door and window frames, painted panelling.

Model Enamel (Gloss, matt and satin finish) Ornaments and accessories, doorsteps, fireplaces. A few drops can be used as a mixer with emulsion paint.

Gouache (from suppliers of artists' materials) A small amount mixed with emulsion paint and then diluted with a splash of water will produce glowing colours for walls.

Acrylic Can be used as gouache.

Varnish Clear (gloss), matt, semi-matt or coloured. Use varnish formulated for art or craft.

Woodstain Woodstains are useful for fittings and furniture. Wipe on with a dry cloth and use a brush in corners. Can be varnished if shine is wanted.

MAKERS OF FEATURED MINIATURES

BIBLIOGRAPHY

FISHER, Robert E. *Art of Tibet* Thames & Hudson, 1997, pbk

GANTZHORN, Volkmar. *Oriental Carpets* Taschen, 1998

GAYNOR, Elizabeth, HAAVISTO Kari & GOLDSTEIN Darra. *Russian Houses* Taschen, 1994

HITCHMOUGH, Wendy. *The Arts & Crafts Home* Pavilion Books, 2000

JACOBSON, Dawn. *Chinoiserie* Phaidon 1993, ppbk, 1999

LASDUN, Susan. *Victorians at Home* Weidenfeld & Nicholson 1981, ppbk, 1985

LOVATT-SMITH, Lisa. *Moroccan Interiors.* Taschen

MILLER, Judith and Martin *Period Details* Mitchell Beazley, 1987

MOULIN, Pierre, LEVEC, Pierre and DANNENBERG, Linda *French Country* Thames & Hudson, 1984

PARISSIEN, Steven. *Regency Style* Phaidon, 1992

PARISSIEN, Steven. *The Georgian Group Book of the Georgian House* Aurum Press, 1995

SLESIN, Susanne, CLIFF, Stafford and ROZENSZTROCH, Daniel. *Japanese Style* Thames & Hudson, 1993

STONE, Dominic R. *The Art of Biedermeier* Chartwell Books, 1990 (Quintet)

TASCHEN, Angelika (Ed.) *Indian Interiors* Taschen, 1999

WILK, Christopher. *Western Furniture 1350 to the present day* Abbeville Pub. USA 1996, Philip Wilson Britain 1996

WOOD, Margaret. *The English Medieval House* Bracken Books, 1983

YPMA, Herbert J.M. *India Modern* Phaidon, 1994 ppbk. 1997

IMPERIAL & METRIC

The standard dolls' house scale is 1/12, which was originally based on imperial measures: one inch represents one foot. Although many craftspeople now use metric measurements, dolls' house hobbyists in Britain and especially in America still use feet and inches. In this book imperial measures of length are given first, followed by their metric equivalent. Accuracy to the millimetre is generally inappropriate, and metric measurements are often rounded up or down a little for convenience.

Practically all the miniatures in this book are in 1/12 scale.

ACKNOWLEDGEMENTS

I would like to thank Stephanie Horner for her advice and encouragement; Ian Hunt for producing such an attractive design for the book; and especially my editor, David Arscott, for overseeing the project. I would also like to acknowledge the contribution made by my husband, Alec, who took so many photographs with immense patience and enthusiasm for the subject.

Special thanks are due to the many makers who completed miniatures to meet our photographic schedule, and to the suppliers and craftspeople who loaned miniatures for photography: Anglesey Dolls' Houses, Blackwells of Hawkwell, Matthew Damper, Farthingale, Hever Castle Ltd, Honeychurch Toys Ltd, Merry Gourmet Miniatures, Caroline Nevill Miniatures and Colin and Yvonne Roberson.

I would also like to thank those outside the dolls' house hobby who contributed with information and help on specialised subjects on which I based miniature settings: in particular, David Freeman of Bonapartes, for his superb painting skills and for his knowledge of the Napoleonic Wars; Icon Art for allowing me to include pictures from their catalogue and for many interesting discussions on the nature of icons; Tibet Foundation and Tibet Shop for permission to include pictured reproductions of thangkas owned by Riga in my Buddhist setting; and Tharpa Publications for supplying the statue of the Buddha modelled by miniaturist Sue Cook.

And lastly, I am grateful to the miniaturists who provided photographs of their work so that we could include as wide a selection as possible.

PHOTOGRAPHIC ACKNOWLEDGEMENTS

Photographs on the following pages were supplied courtesy of:

Angus Puffins, 61-2, 102
David Betts (Grandads Playroom) 29, 30,
David Booth, 41, 43, 44
Neil Carter, 90, 130
Matthew Damper (photograph by Norman McDonald), 60
John Davenport, 42, 95, 96 (top)
Robert Dawson (The Modelroom), 26, 27
Judith Dunger (photograph by Trevor Dunger), 38

Edinburgh Dolls' House Club, 73
Frances England (England's Magic), 25
Anne Funnell (Lenham Pottery), 76
Hever Castle Ltd, 31, 53, 72
Barry Hipwell, 34, 38, 63, 96 (bottom)
Charlotte Hunt, 8, 10
David Hurley, 97
Elizabeth LePla, ELF, 74 (top)
Carol Lodder, 38, 78
Terry McAlister, 129
Alan McKirdy, 45, 81, 98, 99
Peter Mattison, frontispiece, 2, 8, 24, 74(bottom), 137

Midland Miniaturists Association (photograph by Ray Shimell), 60
Mulvany & Rogers, 1, 3, 28, 37, 101
Brian Nickolls, Dolphin Miniatures, 79
Patrick Puttock, 41
Gill Rawling, Petite Fleur, 52
Harry Saunders, Daydream Dwellings, 26 (bottom)
Ivan Turner, 97
Michael Walton, 100
Paul Wells (photographs by Paul Dane), 25, 39, 40
Geoffrey Wonnacott, 98, 99

ABOUT THE AUTHOR

Jean Nisbett began to take notice of period houses, their decoration and furniture, before she was ten years old, and they have been a consuming passion ever since. She turned this interest to the miniature scale while bringing up a family.

Her work has been shown on BBC Television, Channel 4 and TF1 France. She began writing while working in the London offices of an American advertising agency, and she is well known as the leading British writer in the dolls' house field. Her articles have appeared regularly in the specialist dolls' house magazines since 1985, as well as in home decoration magazines. This is her fifth book for GMC Publications.

Jean is president of MinTA, the Miniaturists' Trade Association. She lives in Bath, Somerset.

INDEX

TITLES AVAILABLE FROM

GMC PUBLICATIONS

BOOKS

WOODCARVING

The Art of the Woodcarver	GMC Publications
Carving Architectural Detail in Wood: The Classical Tradition	Frederick Wilbur
Carving Birds & Beasts	GMC Publications
Carving the Human Figure: Studies in Wood and Stone	Dick Onians
Carving Nature: Wildlife Studies in Wood	Frank Fox-Wilson
Carving Realistic Birds	David Tippey
Decorative Woodcarving	Jeremy Williams
Elements of Woodcarving	Chris Pye
Essential Woodcarving Techniques	Dick Onians
Further Useful Tips for Woodcarvers	GMC Publications
Lettercarving in Wood: A Practical Course	Chris Pye
Making & Using Working Drawings for Realistic Model Animals	Basil F. Fordham
Power Tools for Woodcarving	David Tippey
Practical Tips for Turners & Carvers	GMC Publications
Relief Carving in Wood: A Practical Introduction	Chris Pye
Understanding Woodcarving	GMC Publications
Understanding Woodcarving in the Round	GMC Publications
Useful Techniques for Woodcarvers	GMC Publications
Wildfowl Carving – Volume 1	Jim Pearce
Wildfowl Carving – Volume 2	Jim Pearce
Woodcarving: A Complete Course	Ron Butterfield
Woodcarving: A Foundation Course	Zoë Gertner
Woodcarving for Beginners	GMC Publications
Woodcarving Tools & Equipment Test Reports	GMC Publications
Woodcarving Tools, Materials & Equipment	Chris Pye

WOODTURNING

Adventures in Woodturning	David Springett
Bert Marsh: Woodturner	Bert Marsh
Bowl Turning Techniques Masterclass	Tony Boase
Colouring Techniques for Woodturners	Jan Sanders
Contemporary Turned Wood: New Perspectives in a Rich Tradition	Ray Leier, Jan Peters & Kevin Wallace
The Craftsman Woodturner	Peter Child
Decorative Techniques for Woodturners	Hilary Bowen
Fun at the Lathe	R.C. Bell
Illustrated Woodturning Techniques	John Hunnex
Intermediate Woodturning Projects	GMC Publications
Keith Rowley's Woodturning Projects	Keith Rowley
Practical Tips for Turners & Carvers	GMC Publications
Turning Green Wood	Michael O'Donnell
Turning Miniatures in Wood	John Sainsbury
Turning Pens and Pencils	Kip Christensen & Rex Burningham

Understanding Woodturning	Ann & Bob Phillips
Useful Techniques for Woodturners	GMC Publications
Useful Woodturning Projects	GMC Publications
Woodturning: Bowls, Platters, Hollow Forms, Vases, Vessels, Bottles, Flasks, Tankards, Plates	GMC Publications
Woodturning: A Foundation Course (New Edition)	Keith Rowley
Woodturning: A Fresh Approach	Robert Chapman
Woodturning: An Individual Approach	Dave Regester
Woodturning: A Source Book of Shapes	John Hunnex
Woodturning Jewellery	Hilary Bowen
Woodturning Masterclass	Tony Boase
Woodturning Techniques	GMC Publications
Woodturning Tools & Equipment Test Reports	GMC Publications
Woodturning Wizardry	David Springett

WOODWORKING

Advanced Scrollsaw Projects	GMC Publications
Bird Boxes and Feeders for the Garden	Dave Mackenzie
Complete Woodfinishing	Ian Hosker
David Charlesworth's Furniture-Making Techniques	David Charlesworth
The Encyclopedia of Joint Making	Terrie Noll
Furniture & Cabinetmaking Projects	GMC Publications
Furniture-Making Projects for the Wood Craftsman	GMC Publications
Furniture-Making Techniques for the Wood Craftsman	GMC Publications
Furniture Projects	Rod Wales
Furniture Restoration (Practical Crafts)	Kevin Jan Bonner
Furniture Restoration and Repair for Beginners	Kevin Jan Bonner
Furniture Restoration Workshop	Kevin Jan Bonner
Green Woodwork	Mike Abbott
Kevin Ley's Furniture Projects	Kevin Ley
Making & Modifying Woodworking Tools	Jim Kingshott
Making Chairs and Tables	GMC Publications
Making Classic English Furniture	Paul Richardson
Making Little Boxes from Wood	John Bennett
Making Screw Threads in Wood	Fred Holder
Making Shaker Furniture	Barry Jackson
Making Woodwork Aids and Devices	Robert Wearing
Mastering the Router	Ron Fox
Minidrill: Fifteen Projects	John Everett
Pine Furniture Projects for the Home	Dave Mackenzie
Practical Scrollsaw Patterns	John Everett
Router Magic: Jigs, Fixtures and Tricks to Unleash your Router's Full Potential	Bill Hylton
Routing for Beginners	Anthony Bailey
The Scrollsaw: Twenty Projects	John Everett
Sharpening: The Complete Guide	Jim Kingshott
Sharpening Pocket Reference Book	Jim Kingshott
Simple Scrollsaw Projects	GMC Publications
Space-Saving Furniture Projects	Dave Mackenzie